Wave Walkers

When Belief Becomes Faith

Mark W. Roberts

Foreword by

Dr. Greg Ammons

Wave Walkers – When Belief Becomes Faith

Table of Contents

Foreword

Undoubtedly, it was one of those moments from Scripture that you wished you would have been there to witness for yourself. Well, that is now that we know how the story ended. I am not certain that we would have wanted to be in the boat in a storm on the Sea of Galilee if we did not know how the story ends. However, we know how the story ends. It ended, as did many of Jesus' narratives, with the miraculous. Jesus walked on the water to the disciples. But why? Can we do the same or was that a once in a lifetime event?

Wave walking happened very early in Jesus' ministry, sandwiched between the feeding of the 5,000 with five loaves and two fish and other healings in Gennesaret. I wonder why this powerful, life-changing event took place so early in Jesus' ministry? Even Job, years earlier, stated that Jesus was capable of this. *"Who alone spreads out the heavens and walks upon the waves of the sea?"* (Job 9:8).

There may be a few reasons as to why Jesus walked among the waves at this point in His ministry. Perhaps to ensure the disciples and those who followed Him that the Savior truly is in control and in charge over everything. It was a part of His sovereignty. The late Bible scholars Merrill Tenney and Dwight Pentecost believed that the event highlighted Jesus' relationship with His disciples.

They state that the incident was specifically designed to instruct the apostles and increase their faith. Other scholars believe that Jesus walked on the waves in order to assert His divinity and establish this fact among early Christians. Authority over water, especially in the Semitic mindset, would attest to Jesus' deity.

No doubt, the event was etched in the minds of the disciples and early believers, but what does it mean for us? In the book you are holding, *Wave Walkers*, my friend Mark W. Roberts does an amazing job of showing you how. He does not bury this powerful incident in the pages of history but allows it to come alive for us today. Perhaps you can feel the spray of the sea as you read through the pages.

The subtitle of *Wave Walkers* is "*Where Belief Becomes Faith*." In this work, Roberts makes an apt distinction between these two theological truths. Often, we have believed in Jesus Christ as the only Savior of the world and submitted to Him our life, but do we place our faith in Him in the crucible of life? Do we demonstrate faith in Jesus when the storm begins to howl?

Throughout the book, the author focuses on this one event of our Lord walking on the sea and allows us to peruse it from various angles. Roberts masterfully sets the stage in the initial chapters. Next, he details some of the disciples and how they must have responded. Peter, Andrew, Jude, Nathanael, Philip, James, John, and Judas are all examined carefully. The author also notes the seeming risk that was involved to all.

Interspersed throughout *Wave Walkers* are poignant historical facts, such as the discovery of the Jesus Boat on the shores of the Sea of Galilee in 1986. I was privileged to view this amazing find in a museum on a recent trip to Israel. Roberts also provides keen insight into many aspects of the wave walking event, from both a personal viewpoint and those of noted commentators. Overall, this book is well-researched and presented in an interesting, readable format.

One of the strengths of Wave Walkers is that the author does not leave the event buried in the pages of history. He draws personal application for each of us to walk waves, following our Lord, as well.

Roberts encourages the reader to study Scripture and the life of Jesus for yourself. Then, he closes with pertinent personal application. In Chapter 20, the writer declared, *"Jesus cared for them and He cares for you."*

I have studied the passages of Jesus' wave walking carefully for many years. I hold an undergraduate theology degree from Oklahoma Baptist University as well as masters and doctoral degrees from Southwestern Baptist Theological Seminary.

I have served as pastor of three churches for more than 30 years and have preached from these passages many times. In addition, I have taught theology in universities, at both undergraduate and doctoral levels, for many years as well. Several of these courses have dealt with the wave walking of our Lord.

I have known Mark W. Roberts well for the past 14 years. Mark and his family are faithful members of the First Baptist Church of Garland, Texas, where I serve as the Senior Pastor. I have worked with Mark in various settings, including his service as a deacon and Sunday School teacher in our congregation. I

n addition, Mark has led out in worship on our Praise Team, served on our First Impressions Team, and been involved in our Men's Ministry. He has strong theological insight from his matriculation days at Liberty University and then years of study of God's Word. Previously, he wrote an impactful book entitled, *Going the Speed Limit.*

So, grab a cup of coffee, turn on a lamp, and settle in to enjoy the *Wave Walkers* experience. See what the disciples saw. Feel what they felt. Experience what they experienced bobbing along in 80 feet of water on the Sea of Galilee. Maybe you will even feel the breeze as the wind begins to kick up and the waves begin to crest.

Learn to trust in Jesus as they learned to trust Him. The book closes by stating, *"The believers finally believed."* May you as well. May you finally believe in Jesus as the disciples believed on that unforgettable day in northern Galilee.

Dr. Greg Ammons, Senior Pastor
First Baptist Church, Garland, Texas

Preface

Searching the Scriptures for a story to tell for Believers is like being a kid let loose in a candy store without limits. You can choose whatever sugary delight you wish, and as much as your arms can carry, all at no charge. The hardest thing you have to do is figure out where to start. After you get going, the rest is easy. You simply pick up what speaks to you and what you feel are the best pieces to consume at that time.

Stories about Jesus have been told for two thousand years. He is the One about whom the church has heard since He walked the earth during His lifetime. Upon His death, the followers of the Way, which is how early Believers were called, exploded in number during Roman persecution. His disciples were found all over the known world, and many stories were told about Him in oral tradition in the beginning days of the church.

However, most of what is known about the Life of Christ comes from writings by His apostles—those men who were closest to Him during his three and a half year ministry before He was crucified. They recorded many of their life events with Jesus and stories of His miracles, His teaching and conversations with them, and His sermons and parables.

Additional non-Biblical works attribute more information about Jesus and his disciples, and some of those works are more credible than others. There are historical documents that detail stories about Him from historians such as Flavius Josephus and Cornelius Tacitus who both lived in the first century. These two among others have stood the test of time and are the most closely related in the time frame when Jesus was alive and the stories of His disciples. It is even possible that they were able to talk with some of them.

Their writings give the best and most accurate accounts of a historical Jesus, and they have been commonly accepted for 1,900 years as truthful documentation of life in that era, especially dealing with any aspects of the Roman government and its interaction with the Jewish people. They each offer strong evidence of His historicity as compared to a purely mythological creation of early Christians. There is no doubt that Jesus did exist as a real person.

As well, early church fathers such as Ignatius of Antioch and Clement of Rome wrote extensively about their knowledge of Jesus. Bible scholars accept that Clement was personally acquainted with both Peter and the Apostle Paul. Their influence on him was notable, and the writings he produced have been considered authentic since he lived in the first century.

Ignatius was very highly regarded as a historian of the early church in the second century, and he produced an abundance of letters to churches convincing them of the man called Jesus and His divine nature. He was a martyr for his faith.

One additional aspect of truth in the life of Jesus and his disciples is supported by archeological evidence. Every area where they lived and walked has been excavated, and physical proof has been well documented about locations and individuals who were mentioned in the scriptures, including Pontius Pilate. Physical proof does not lie. But belief in a historical Jesus is just the starting point for faith.

It is not the head knowledge that saves an individual from eternal separation from God. The heart must believe.

When Jesus began His public ministry as an adult, He was immediately recognized by his contemporaries as extraordinary and sent from God. His cousin John the Baptist pointed that fact out on first sight. Jesus was able to build a following of disciples rather quickly after He was baptized and then began calling out those He wished to have in His inner circle, the twelve men who would follow Him for the next three and a half years until His crucifixion. After that experience, it took the disciples a little while longer to realize their real mission on Earth – about 40 days more.

Miracles were performed by Jesus during His earthly ministry, and the disciples were there to witness them firsthand. They struggled with the knowledge of accepting Jesus as the Messiah, primarily because their religious customs and traditions were based on a false understanding of what his role was expected to be. Additionally, they as a group were always grumbling about their individual responsibilities as disciples and followers of the Christ.

These dozen men that Jesus hand selected were very human in their daily struggles. They were selfish, and unbelieving, and even fearful. Much of the interaction between the disciples and Jesus was about them questioning His authority, and Jesus trying to teach them about Himself and God.

The relationship between the disciples and Jesus was one of trust, but often these men would argue amongst themselves about the meaning of life. They would question why he made certain statements, and even when Jesus used stories to teach them they still wouldn't get it.

During the events of a particular night on one of their particularly exhausting journeys with Jesus, He would put them into a situation that defied all common logic to show these men who He was and to help them come closer to acknowledging His divinity. Matthew's gospel provides the most detailed account of the extreme miracle of Jesus walking on water on the Sea of Galilee.

The miracle of Jesus walking on water is found in Matthew 14:22-34, Mark 6:45-53, and John 6:15-21. The idea of a powerful person possessing the ability to walk on water was not original when the Gospels were written. It is usually presented in historical texts from earlier times in statements which recognize the act as being just sheerly impossible. Jesus, though, when He walked on the surface of the lake showed his power over nature as a divine attribute, and there were twelve witnesses.

In chapter fourteen of the New Testament Book of Matthew, he unfolds the tale of a very unique event. Jesus would perform His greatest miracle to date, and they would be dumbfounded, fearfully hysterical, and unbelieving – until He calmed their fears with just a few simple words.

The disciples that night were given an order by their Master to launch out across the lake without Him, and that He would see them on the other side. It was their responsibility to go, even if they were not that interested in going. They had developed a significant dependency on Jesus, and to head out at night on the water was somewhat disconcerting and uncertain.

Still, He gave them a command, and they begrudgingly agreed to obey it. Soon, they would experience a situation they had never before faced, and it would further define their relationship with one another and with Jesus.

Peter, the most outspoken of the bunch, put his faith in Jesus when he place himself in mortal danger of drowning. But he was saved, physically at the time and spiritually at a later date. The other disciples did not have the same encounter, but their presence at the scene provided a greater element of faith after it occurred.

They all realized that something monumentally unreal and unusual had just taken place, and they saw it with their own tired and bleary eyes. They were not dreaming or having visions, nor were they so ridiculously fatigued that they imagined it was unfolding in front of them in spite of all their common sense that it should not be happening.

Since that event was recorded, there have been scoffers and skeptics who don't accept the validity of the gospel accounts by any of the disciples. Even more so today, two thousand years after the fact, the doubters exist in the billions, including many who would consider themselves Christians.

Not all are in agreement over how to interpret the story of Jesus walking on water. Some see the event as mythical and symbolic, rather than a literal event. Should Believers give more importance to Jesus and the disciples than on the actual details of the miracle itself?

What about Peter's actions and the plight of the rest of the men on board the tiny boat? What should Christians think about what Jesus told the disciples once He was on board after calming the wind and water? Did this story really happen, or was it a parable created by the writers to show their belief in Jesus and convince their readers He was, indeed, the Messiah?

The Bible emphatically states that all scripture is God inspired and God breathed.

He was the author of the Word from Genesis to Revelation, and He used men to write it all down. Believers are taught to accept this as fact. Yet many doubt. They pick and choose what they want to believe, and disregard what they disagree with in order to justify a lifestyle. But what is faith? What is belief? What is worship of God?

This event in the gospel record is about acknowledging who God is by praising Him for both who He is and for what He has done. It was in this story found in Matthew Chapter 14 that the disciples took their first step and worshiped Jesus as the Son of God.

This book has been written to provide you as the reader a practical idea of the propensity of the event, and to learn more about the actors on this stage set in Israel two thousand years ago. The lessons Jesus taught the disciples, especially during the event under discussion, are still being taught today to those who would be called Christian, and as a way to provide one more evidential reason why non-Believers should put their trust in Jesus as Savior.

Chapter One – The Stage is Set

How do you know when your faith is tested? Is it when you encounter difficult circumstances, or you begin to doubt your relationship with the One who created you? Have you experienced seasons in your life that you were uncertain about what the future holds, or what you were going to do next in a particular situation?

Was there ever a time in your life that you committed your life to an Almighty Being greater than yourself? What was the occasion that brought you to a believing faith in God? If you have never trusted in the One who creates, sustains, and delivers life, then you have some deep thinking to do. Much of the material you are about to read may not make any sense to you.

Even Believers have a hard time at times believing in a supernatural source more powerful than life itself.

If you never have given your life to that Person, then now is the time to do it before you read any more words on this page. To trust in Jesus Christ as your personal Lord and Savior is the most important act you can ever do, and to delay action on it is like playing spiritual Russian roulette. The Bible is clear in its definition of faith and salvation, and your eternal destiny is all wrapped up in that one single decision. To ignore it is folly, and to accept it is more than you can ever imagine.

If you are reading this book and need to make that personal choice to accept Him into your life and heart, then turn immediately to the end of this book, after the Epilogue, and read out loud as a prayer to God the Father the words so clearly written to explain what to say to Him. Talk to Him as if He is no longer a stranger but your best friend.

Now, for everyone else who is a Christian—born again by faith in Christ through the power of His saving blood shed on Calvary—

think about how you can insert yourself into the story now to be told. Think about the words in Matthew's gospel that talk about the importance of both salvation and faith. Consider what you would do if you were in the same situation as the apostles.

The premise of this book is based upon a few New Testament verses found in the Book of Matthew. It tells the story that almost every person who has gone to Sunday school as a child or adult, or has listened to sermons in their church services over time have heard at least once.

The lesson taught in scripture and penned by Matthew is both about salvation and faith, and singly one cannot exist without the other for Christians. These two concepts are intertwined in humanity and divine nature, and to separate them does injustice to each. It is impossible to have one and not the other and be truly a child of God.

Salvation is only possible through a personal relationship in God the Son, and His Spirit indwells the Believer, linking inseparably to God the Father. All other world religions may claim a path to Heaven, but as the Bible says "there is no other name whereby you can be saved." Period. End of story. Time to go home. If you have experienced the saving redemptive grace of God then you know this to be true. If not, then you have lost everything.

So then the next step is to learn how this happens and begin to understand what takes place during the process of believing, receiving, and living as a Believer. How does a ragtag group of men from a non-descript part of Judea learn to trust in an itinerant rabbi? And what makes Jesus so popular? The disciples who follow Him are not really initially convinced of his divine attributes, but they come to learn over time how He was able to show and teach them about both salvation and faith.

Granted, like you and everyone else you probably know, being slow to learn truth is something you can admit to be guilty of to some extent. So, don't criticize His boat crew for being any less teachable. To throw them overboard during a time of terrible storm in their lives would be to also include yourself with the crowd.

Read these words as written almost two millennia ago by a former tax collector. Here was a man hated by his community because as a Hebrew he decided to help the Roman government collect their greedy taxes from the community where he lived. Usually, tax collectors were viewed by almost everyone as turncoats—traitors to their people and their religion. Matthew likely was no different, until the day that Jesus stopped at his table in the marketplace and said just two words: "Follow Me."

But the miracle included in these few words are more than a suspension of physical properties. Life is seen by one of the twelve, Peter in particular, as short lived had he not called out for help. To learn how his faith grows, and his salvation experience develops, you need to cry out for your own understanding of God's Word.

Matthew 14:22-33 from the New International Version (NIV):

[22] Immediately Jesus made the disciples get into the boat and go on ahead of him to the other side, while he dismissed the crowd. [23] After he had dismissed them, he went up on a mountainside by himself to pray. Later that night, he was there alone, [24] and the boat was already a considerable distance from land, buffeted by the waves because the wind was against it.

[25] Shortly before dawn Jesus went out to them, walking on the lake. [26] When the disciples saw him walking on the lake, they were terrified. "It's a ghost," they said, and cried out in fear.

[27] But Jesus immediately said to them: "Take courage! It is I. Don't be afraid."

[28] "Lord, if it's you," Peter replied, "tell me to come to you on the water."

[29] "Come," he said.

Then Peter got down out of the boat, walked on the water and came toward Jesus. [30] But when he saw the wind, he was afraid and, beginning to sink, cried out, "Lord, save me!"

[31] Immediately Jesus reached out his hand and caught him. "You of little faith," he said, "why did you doubt?"

32 And when they climbed into the boat, the wind died down. 33 Then those who were in the boat worshiped him, saying, "Truly you are the Son of God."

Mark's Version – Mark 6:45-52:

45 Immediately Jesus made his disciples get into the boat and go on ahead of him to Bethsaida, while he dismissed the crowd. 46 After leaving them, he went up on a mountainside to pray.

47 Later that night, the boat was in the middle of the lake, and he was alone on land. 48 He saw the disciples straining at the oars, because the wind was against them. Shortly before dawn he went out to them, walking on the lake. He was about to pass by them, 49 but when they saw him walking on the lake, they thought he was a ghost. They cried out, 50 because they all saw him and were terrified.

Immediately he spoke to them and said, "Take courage! It is I. Don't be afraid." 51 Then he climbed into the boat with them, and the wind died down. They were completely amazed, 52 for they had not understood about the loaves; their hearts were hardened.

John's Version – John 6:16-21:

16 When evening came, his disciples went down to the lake, 17 where they got into a boat and set off across the lake for Capernaum. By now it was dark, and Jesus had not yet joined them. 18 A strong wind was blowing and the waters grew rough.

19 When they had rowed about three or four miles,[a] they saw Jesus approaching the boat, walking on the water; and they were frightened. 20 But he said to them, "It is I; don't be afraid."

21 Then they were willing to take him into the boat, and immediately the boat reached the shore where they were heading.

These three versions of the same story each indicate the divine nature of the Christ. However, only Matthew goes further into the details about Peter's experience with Jesus. The other two disciples focus solely on the miracle of Jesus walking on the waves across the lake deep in the night. This firsthand account by Matthew is geared for his Jewish audience where their faith lacked belief in who Jesus claimed to be. It was his way of saying, "Jesus is God."

In this short story, the elements of fear, death, and hope are all realized. If you are true to yourself, at some point you have dealt with one or all of these issues. Every single person ever to have walked on earth has been afraid of someone or some thing at one point in his/her life.

Fear can cripple you physically and emotionally, and fear can cause hysteria even on a mass scale. Fear can be deadly. Phobias are exaggerated fear, and hysteria is fear out of control.

And no one has ever not had some hope of some kind—whether for more money or material gain, position or authority, power, relationships, better health or a better life—hope is what drives most people. Some call it the desire for success, and many feel it is the lack of failure. Every man, woman and child has hope, or did at one time. When hope fades, then so does life.

For those without a secure eternal perspective and divine destination, fear of death is overwhelming.

Death is the great equalizer; and at some point you are going to die, or you know someone who has died. Death is a fact of life, ever since Adam and Eve were tossed from the Garden of Eden. When the first couple were found guilty of sin and confessed their misdeeds, God gave death the chance to begin its ugly deteriorating process. All of creation suffered, and still does today. What was deemed good became unlovely.

The story of twelve men in a boat at night in the middle of a stormy lake is more than the old nursery rhyme of "Rub a dub dub, three men in a tub." If you have ever been on a military ship at sea as navy personnel or a cruise ship passenger, you know that the sea can be cruel at times. And, if you've ever been out on a lake in a small sailboat or other type of watercraft when a storm blows in, you probably have experienced some of the same emotions that the apostles did that night on the Sea of Galilee.

That body of water is a large, deep lake surrounded by hills. It can be at times as smooth as glass with no ripples on the water's surface, and it can also be a roiling tumultuous body of water that has been guilty of creating havoc for anyone caught out on it during a storm. For thousands of years, the stories of life on the water there have been well known and well documented. Galileans know the lake, and they fear it when it gets rough.

In this particular case, the event didn't necessarily start out bad, but it quickly turned that way. One noteworthy observation is that Jesus wanted his close band of followers to learn a lesson. Sending them out on a small boat at night on water that has the reputation of getting ugly fast was likely not foremost on their minds that evening. However, they learned more that night about trust than all the other nights combined leading up to what was to be incredible moments of both disbelief and belief.

In the following chapters, this meaningful Bible story is going to be dissected for you to learn more about both salvation and faith. How does this event turn out for the major players, and how it can affect your life is what you can learn, observe, understand, and believe. Not every person who reads this book is going to have the same epiphany, or certainly have the same conclusion. The most important aspect of the story is that it happened for a purpose.

God never does anything by accident. His actions always have meaning, and His timing is perfect. He is intentional in all He does. He is on time – every time.

The story of Jesus and the disciples on the Sea of Galilee is not only about what lessons they learned that night, but also what lessons you can learn from the application of its words and meaning in your life. Put yourself in the boat that fateful night. Imagine your thoughts as you participate as a disciple.

In the eternal weight of following Jesus, how would you have reacted as this wild, windy and wet adventure unfolded? Would your faith be abandoned or strengthened? Whom would you have told about it afterwards? Would you have written a letter or a book about your walk with this phenom known as Jesus?

God had set the stage for one of the single most miraculous events ever recorded in human history. He chose those whom His Son regarded as faithful and who were ready to risk it all. Jesus was about to show them and tell them who He really was. Walking on waves doesn't come easy…unless you are divine. Battling storms usually happens on a regular basis in the lives of just about everyone who draws the breath of life.

These twelve men, and most importantly the one called Peter, were divinely appointed to live through both a physical and spiritual storm. And, having survived this one, they would experience many more for the rest of their lives. What about you? How strong is your faith to survive the storms that are going to come your way? It is said that if you haven't been through one, or are in one now, you are going to go through one at some point in your life.

Chapter Two — The Risk

Imagine that you and your associates were told by your boss one day that you need to go on a little boat ride across the lake from where you had just spent a hard day at work. You're tired and not sure what's happening for the rest of the day into that night, but all you know is that you've been given an order to go out on the lake to get to another location for the next day.

At some point, you get sleepy and want to take some time for a nap on the boat, but the wind kicks up after it gets dark, and you have to get busy getting to the nearest shore. If not, it's possible that a storm is brewing and you don't want to be caught out in the middle of the lake, especially at night. What are you thinking? How much longer is it going to take to get to the other side, and why didn't our Master come with us?

It's a little unlikely that you're all going to break out into a rousing chorus of "Row, row, row your boat" as fun as that sounds. And to ease the tension a bit, you probably want to have some entertainment other than watching grown men cry. Should you start off with a joke or a short story about what you did when your family was on vacation in the Sinai? Or, should you think of what you and each one of your comrades are doing after this gig?

This is no band of merry men. Each of the men in your group was handpicked by someone who called Himself the Son of Man. What does that mean, and what does He expect you to do as one of His followers? Current day Believers have the luxury of looking back at this event in light of published holy texts, but no one was writing this down as it was happening.

If you were one of the twelve, then you were living life with Jesus as it was taking place real time. There was no Bible, or scripture guide, or even Discipleship for Dummies. The men in that boat on that particular night in history were experiencing life changing events, and one of those occasions was soon to take place that night. At once, the ride of a lifetime would both freak them out and cause them to consider in whom they should put their faith and belief.

After all, the common consensus of most believing Jews at the time was that a Messiah would come to deliver the nation of Israel and set Himself up as the reigning monarch. These men were fully committed to make that happen, but in the meantime they had hitched their wagon (or the proverbial donkey cart) to a man who they still were puzzled by and trying to figure out. Could He be the One, this Jesus of Nazareth?

Your task is to follow directions, but this set of instructions seems to be a bit crazy. Get into a boat and go to the other side of the lake, but wait for your leader. Wait where—the lake, the shore, the boat, the inn in town? For men who were used to having specific tasks or livelihoods, this errand seemed to be a bit unorthodox. Maybe even a little bit odd.

After all, who goes out onto the Sea of Galilee at night, unless you're planning on fishing. Tax collectors only fish for money from tax payers. The writer of the verses in the first chapter of this book was not a fisherman. He was used to being on land, not water.

Jesus could see them, even from a distance. He is completely human and divine at the same time, and His men were getting into trouble…again. He knew they would need Him, and He sent them on this very interesting journey out over the deep waters so He could show them something about believing. He also knew that unless He delivered them, His little band of brothers would be in grave peril.

Some of the disciples fished for a living. How can the men who were familiar with being out on the water and who were used to handling boats and the waves be put into such fear of their lives? Come on, now. Some of these guys made their living by being on the water most of their lives up to this point. After all, how much damage could a little bit of wind do to their mini-cruise?

Fear is a powerful tool in the hands of the enemy, and faith can weaken when your focus is not on the intended target.

Jesus already had a plan in mind before He asked them to go out in the boat. He wanted His disciples to learn to trust Him and in Him. But they weren't ready to commit to that level of trust just yet. The disciples' unbridled zeal to serve their Messiah waned greatly when they thought that they were in danger. Jesus was very aware of the gravity of their situation, and He prepared to teach them all a valuable lesson about faith.

To quote a line from a 1994 television episode of Seinfeld: "The sea was angry that day my friends, like an old man trying to return soup at a deli!" As funny as that line sounds, the truth is that the men on the Galilee were in the same predicament as many who had gone before them, and in peril for their sanity and safety.

Indeed, the twelve were in rough water. John's Gospel account of this event has less narrative but provides a bit more insight into their situation that night:

John 6:16-21 New International Version (NIV): *"[16] When evening came, his disciples went down to the lake,*

[17] where they got into a boat and set off across the lake for Capernaum. By now it was dark, and Jesus had not yet joined them. [18] A strong wind was blowing and the waters grew rough.

[19] When they had rowed about three or four miles, they saw Jesus approaching the boat, walking on the water; and they were frightened. [20] But he said to them, "It is I; don't be afraid."

[21] Then they were willing to take him into the boat, and immediately the boat reached the shore where they were heading."

The Greek word "stadia" that was used in the original text means that the measurement was about 185 yards times twenty-five or thirty—roughly three to four miles or so. The rowing was undoubtedly wearing them out as they have been dealing with this precocious windstorm all night long. Not only were they out in the middle of the lake, they were having difficulty making any headway at all due to the inclement weather.

Another observation about John's text is that he identifies where they were headed, and how soon they arrived after Jesus showed up to greet them on the water---it was immediate. Another lesson to be more fully explored later is that the risk was over when the Master arrived. In your life, is that a common occurrence; do you fret about whether He is going to show up on time?

The disciples were trying to get back home where Jesus and some of the apostles lived in Capernaum, located at the northern tip of the Galilean Sea. Have you ever been on a trip trying to get to a destination, or traveling to get back home, when you suffer delay after delay and just cannot get there when you want or need to arrive? If you've ever been an airport traveler, you know their pain, only on a scale that is far greater than a little bit of luggage carousel roulette.

Imagine the feeling of being in this predicament at night in a small boat in the middle of a lake. Now imagine no cell phones, GPS, or radios to get you help. It's just you and the boat and wind, plus your pals in the boat that are sitting next to you. Talk about a team effort. All these gentlemen rowing to get to shore, and it ain't happenin.'

John doesn't give a lot of detail about this event, but says that it was at least noteworthy to mention in his story about his life with Jesus. He may have thought that after the feeding of the five thousand earlier that day that another miracle was just what he expected from the Christ. It's hard to tell what may have been going on in his mind that night, but whatever he felt about the ride across Galilee's Sea was pale in comparison to what he experienced with the loaves and fishes that he helped pass out.

Granted, you don't usually see someone walking on water every day. John was probably more in tune with Jesus than most of the other disciples, but he was undoubtedly blown away more by his time with Him than with some errant nocturnal wind storm. The fourth watch is defined by the Roman watch as a time spanning from 3am – 6am. Sometime before dawn, the apostles were still struggling to get to the other side of the lake, and when Jesus showed up, they had already been vigorously contending with this storm for most of the night. Considering this was nine hours after sunset, the sun was likely about to come up on them-that's a really long night.

Additionally, these men were at the time no different than most of the Jewish population regarding superstitions. Many stories and legends about spirits and ghosts were commonly believed in those days, even among the Jews. Not much has changed since then when it comes to people believing in the supernatural. They likely remembered the ancient Hebrew story about King Saul consulting with a witch to bring back the spirit of Samuel from the dead. That would give anyone the shivers.

Seeing someone walking on the water in the dead of night would have definitely struck terror in their hearts. They cried out in fear anticipating they would be taken one by one to Sheol, the denizen of the damned. No doubt, each of the disciples were very concerned for their lives at the moment. Would they drown? Would they lose their immortal souls? Would this spirit curse them forever? Would their lives be over before the sun came up? If you had been there, would you have had the same thoughts racing through your mind? Probably.

The water world that Jesus walked upon was a perfect stage for the story about twelve men in need of faith, and a Savior that strode out to meet their needs. At one point it appeared that He was actually on His way to the other side to meet them, but then took compassion on them due to their struggle and their fear. Mark's Gospel says that Jesus was about to pass them by when He heard them scream in fright.

Imagine Jesus moving effortlessly against the wind on top of the water in the middle of the night just to be ready for His disciples to meet Him where He had told them to go. He had already planned to be there waiting on these men to show up.

Divinity has no boundaries in time and space.

Humanity is beholden to them, but in Jesus' case His supernatural abilities overrode the natural elements that would bind normal men.

The question about why this took place has long been one that has puzzled mankind. What was the purpose of this account written by three of the four gospel writers? Why would Jesus make a point of showing Himself in this situation? Who would benefit from knowing about what happened that night besides the disciples? These men were simple and superstitious. Frankly, none of them were that intelligent outside of their own crafts. They were not learned men, nor were they known to be. At best, they understood tasks, but not much more.

The plain fact is that the purpose of Jesus' walking on water had nothing to do with going on a trip across the Sea of Galilee. Simply, it had everything to do with the audience who would read his message. The disciples lived in a culture where there were many stories about people who claimed ownership of some element of divinity. One common feature of having divine powers was the ability to walk on water. Those who claimed they could just never performed the task with an audience to witness the feat.

Jesus walked on water because He had to walk on water. He had to show who He really was to them and to the world. If He hadn't performed this one extreme miracle, it would have been difficult for the early Christians to insist that their Son of God was just as powerful as other men who claimed to be a god. He meant for them to see Him, in spite of the wind and the waves and all the other external forces that were bearing down on them.

In spite of the lack of faith and the innate fear of the unknown, Jesus meant for the disciples to know Him. Jesus walking on the water isn't just showing off that He can do miracles. He wasn't just showing these men that He was God just because He could walk on water. He was allowing the disciples to see His glory as He passed by them. Not only that, He was proclaiming to them His name – He essentially told them He is the great "I am." All of these guys, even the toughest among them, would have understood the meaning of that phrase. What Jesus was doing was revealing His divinity to the disciples, even when their hearts were hardened.

As they proceeded to the shore and landed as the scripture says immediately after Jesus entered the boat, Peter and the rest of this rag tag group knew something unique and highly unusual had just happened. They had been witnesses to something that seemed incredible to believe and difficult to understand, yet they all knew that they had personally encountered God.

Faith and belief were beginning to meld together, yet each of these men still needed more of both. At the right time in the near future for them, they would finally believe in Jesus through their faith in Him except for the one among them who would ultimately fail. In the meantime, the work that Jesus was doing was not yet complete. He knew it, and He knew when it would end. The disciples did not, but they would recognize it later when it happened.

Each man was risking all by following Jesus. They risked their reputations, their livelihoods, their families, their present daily survival, and their future. The Gospels go into some detail about their life and times during their three and a half years with Jesus. They had already seen some miracles, but nothing on the scale of seeing Him casually strolling on the Sea of Galilee.

To walk with Jesus in the miraculous, to know His voice, to recognize His face, to be humbled by His appearance and His words. He was able to turn fear into faith.

How would you have felt to be so close to divine power, yet not really recognize it until the time was almost too late? During the days when the New Testament Gospels were actually being lived out, before any of the actual original texts had even been written, rubbing shoulders with the Messiah would have been the closest to surviving the daily risks of threats of the spiritual corruption displayed openly and secretly by the Jewish religious leaders, the savagery of the Roman government in its desire to control all aspects of everyday life, and the harshness of natural elements where they lived. The disciples knew risk.

Every day you live, you face risk. How do you get through it? How is your faith? Take courage in knowing that the One served by the disciples two thousand years ago is still able to help you manage your fears, your beliefs, and your courage to live through difficult times. When storms come, and the uncertainty of your direction is causing doubt and disbelief, focus on the truth of His promise to keep you safe. Jesus may not remove you from the storm, but He promises to be with you until the end of it. Storms come and go. Some last a short while, and some are seemingly unending.

Regardless of the severity of your storm, Jesus is the solid rock to keep your life from complete shipwreck upon the rocks. Remember His word to the dozen, "Fear not." He says the same to you.

Chapter Three – Water Water Everywhere

Why does the Sea of Galilee hold so much significance in the story about a little stroll at night by a Jewish carpenter turned rabbi and his loud mouthed fisherman friend? As the lowest fresh water lake in the world geographically, it is about 700 feet below sea level. The lake measures about thirteen miles long and a little over eight miles wide. The lake is fed partly by underground springs. However, its main source of water is the Jordan River, which flows through it from north to south.

The Sea of Galilee has an ancient history that stretches back to pre-Roman times and has been called by different names throughout its history, usually depending on the the most settlement on its shores at the time. With the changing situations of the towns, the lake's name also changed. The name Galilee came from an old Hebrew word that means "district."

Prior to that, during the days of Joshua over 3,300 years ago, the lake was known as the Sea of Kinneret, or Sea of Chinnereth, as called in the Old Testament book of Numbers, named after a Bronze Age city by the same name according to some scholars. A common colloquial ancient story says that the name comes from an old word meaning "lyre" which is a very old type of musical stringed harp. The lake has a shape similar to a lyre. No one really knows for sure.

Another old moniker is Sea of Ginosar from an area on the western side of the Lake. The Apostle Luke, who was a Greek, referred to it as the Sea of Gennesaret which is a Greek language version of Kinneret. Finally, because King Herod Antipas had established a city to honor the then Roman Emperor Tiberius built on its shore, the lake has been called the Sea of Tiberius. Regardless of its name, the lake has a reputation.

The peaceful calm of the Sea of Galilee can quickly become transformed by a violent storm. Winds funnel through the east-west aligned Galilee hill country and stir up the waters quickly. More violent are the winds that come off the hills of the Golan Heights to the east. Trapped in the basin, the winds can be deadly to fishermen. That night when Jesus appeared to the disciples was definitely one of those times.

Jesus used the area around the Sea of Galilee as a large part of his public ministry, after his public baptism by John the Baptist. For the next three and a half years, Jesus used its shore an its water as a way to bring people to himself. Because the lake was hugely popular for fishing, it had a large workforce of fishermen who plied their trade there.

Out of those, he chose Peter and his brother Andrew plus James and John as part of his band of twelve closest disciples. He would teach them to become *"fishers of men."* This area called Galilee is the cradle of the gospel. It is the beginning of what later generations would call the Holy Land.

Jesus would use the lake many times to teach his disciples about life, about God, and about Himself. He talked about the importance of surrendering to the will of His Father. At Capernaum, located on the northwest shore, He would bring men to serve with Him. They would come to understand over time His stories, parables and metaphors of spiritual significance. Early in their familiarity with Him, the disciples would not fully comprehend the meaning of much of what Jesus talked about when they were together. It took a while for each of them to grasp the relevance of who Jesus was and what His mission was, and how He would impact them.

That single solitary life would mean more than all they would ever own.

He would teach them there that *"...the kingdom of heaven is like a net that was let down into the lake..."* (Matthew 13:47). The lake served as a backdrop for the miraculous feeding of the 4,000 and the second miracle of the feeding of the 5,000 with only a few loaves of bread and fishes.

When the Gospels record his miraculous catches of fish, those took place at the Sea of Galilee. When Jesus cleansed the demoniac from the Legion of demons, he sent them to the herd of pigs that ran over the cliff into the Sea there. When Jesus reconciled Peter after his denial, and the death and resurrection of Christ, it happened on the shore of the Sea of Galilee.

Because Jesus made his residence in the fishing village of Capernaum during his earthly ministry and traveled the region of the Sea of Galilee, the lives of these real fishing families became the fabric from which He wove many of His stories. Moreover, it was Jesus healing individuals in Galilean villages, or crossing the Sea with His disciples, or sitting in a boat by the shore teaching those who gathered to hear Him speak which were the stories that reflected His desire to reach the people of His community. The Sea of Galilee was His home base, and He used it to His advantage.

This region shaped Jesus from a human perspective, and perhaps that is why He chose this area for His public ministry. Galilee is far removed from the political and religious center of power in Jerusalem. It was blue-collar territory — "everyday" people lived there including fishermen and farmers. When the disciples were called to minister with Him, they didn't have far to travel. For the most part, they lived and worked in an area with great familiarity.

Not only that, they were part of the home crowd. These men related to those with whom they came in contact. And many of them were known as Galileans. People in Galilee worked to survive. It was not an intellectual center. Faith was not a mental exercise for these individuals.

Their faith was an everyday experience they lived out with real consequences.

The disciples, including Peter, knew the value of their hard work and their religion. He would have known the analogies well that Jesus told, and he would have related to the meaning behind them even if it was on a surface level.

Peter took time to come to the realization concerning this Nazarene preacher. He didn't have an immediate grasp of what the Son of Man was saying. Jesus spoke to Peter's inner being when He said that Peter would be a fisher of men. He may not have understood at the time, but after his reconciliation with his risen Savior years later on the beach at breakfast, Peter finally had the epiphany that he had longer for during these years of trial and sacrifice with Christ.

His boldness became bolder in the face of persecution. His preaching was empowered by the Holy Spirit and provided the power to persevere. His humility became more humble when He grasped the depth of what Jesus accomplished on the cross.

The Sea of Galilee experience for Peter was a watershed moment in faith. He learned to trust in someone, and to believe wholeheartedly that there were no other options to live apart from complete dependence on God. Failure to do so would have jeopardized not only his mortal existence but also his eternal destiny. When Peter stepped out of the boat and into the water, he stepped up to a new level of faith even if it was only for a few moments. It was a beginning.

Peter's journey of faith was continuing to grow slowly during the years after he first met Jesus. When the disciples took their orders from the Son of God to go across the Sea of Galilee that night, none of them knew what was going to happen. None of them expected a storm. None of them anticipated they'd be struggling overnight and be physically exhausted after rowing that boat hour after hour for what seemed an endless crossing. And most of all, none of them woke up that morning hoping they would see a ghost coming to them in the wee hours of the dark night.

Peter was the one who showed his courage when death seemed imminent, and survival was critical. The rest of the twelve just sat amazed at the scene that began to unfold in front of them. The disciples all knew that if the boat capsized in the middle of the Sea of Galilee during this storm, they in all probability would not live through the night. The fishermen on board knew that the boat had a high degree of failure if things went wrong during their journey across the lake. They each understood the consequences.

The letter by Matthew does not indicate the time of year when this event happened. He doesn't describe the temperature of the water or the general weather conditions or the nature of how the winds developed to create the situation. He only says that a storm came and buffeted them about with the winds. He doesn't say it was raining or that any other meteorological conditions were taking place. Just wind. But it was beating them up so much that they were not making any progress to their destination.

In Biblical times, there was no radar to provide advance warnings. There were no television stations or social media platforms to broadcast impending cold fronts or changes in atmospheric conditions. There was no satellite imagery from space. There were no computer models to evaluate the potential for danger. There were no meteorologists forecasting what would happen over the following news cycle. Weather just happened. You either survived it or you didn't.

There is a lot of water contained in the Sea of Galilee. Scientists have calculated that there are four billion cubic meters of water in the lake which equals $4km^3$. That translates to almost one trillion gallons (908,082,984,268 gallons to be exact). Today the lake provides thirty percent of Israel's drinking water. If Peter had fallen beneath the waves, he would have drowned.

Jesus would not let that happen. When Peter said "prove it," the Messiah said *"Come."* It was up to Peter to prove Christ wrong, not the other way around. Jesus did not need to prove anything about Himself, or His power, or His presence. As the One who spoke the seas into existence millennia before Peter was even born, He knew the water's consistency.

He is the One who created it from nothing. Jesus was the Word in flesh, and the disciples didn't put two and two together until after Jesus overcame death and sin and Hell itself. At some point in the near future after these two walked on water, these twelve disciples would see Jesus not only as the Messiah, but as God Himself. Between the night on the Sea of Galilee and the day that Jesus ascended to Heaven after His forty days post resurrection, there was a lot more to learn. They were just getting started.

The Sea of Galilee became lessons in faith, belief, and trust. The water was just the object by which they all learned not to fear, but to have faith in the Creator of it. Watching Jesus defy gravity was fearful enough. Unsure of how he was accomplishing this feat was even scarier to the disciples who had never experienced fear like this before. After all, they all lived somewhat simple lives without too much discomfort or difficulty.

They were each simple men who lived simply to exist. When they each decided to follow Jesus, they were beginning the rest of their lives on a significantly greater plane. This night cruise in question was a small part of their journey to serve mankind. They just didn't know it yet. Later on when their individual ministries were forming, each man would remember.

I have had the great privilege to experience being on a boat traveling from one side of the lake to the other, although it was a tour boat built for modern day tourist crowds and definitely larger and sturdier than the one the disciples were in two thousand years ago.

I have sat on the shore by the Sea of Galilee at dusk with a fire built from driftwood to warm our small group, and listen to one of my college professors talk about Jesus and the disciples as if it had just happened. I have put my hands and feet into the edge of the gentle waves lapping at the sand where we sat to hear about faith and fear.

From the perspective by the shoreline, the lake looks huge. From the perspective on the boat, it appears smaller. It can be as smooth as glass, or a violent tempest. Trust me, the lake is wet, and it does not support the weight of any man or woman who decides to walk into it. The laws of nature definitely do not bend or cease to exist just because someone feels inclined to stroll into the Sea of Galilee from any point, either from the shore or from a boat in the middle of it.

Walking on waves doesn't ever happen. Matthew's story gives great insight into who made it happen that one time, and it was only because Jesus held the power of nature in His hand. When the twelve men were dealing with a fierce wind all night, undoubtedly their first thought was to just get to the other side as soon as possible.

Their last thought was how to deal with the sight they experienced that night. How were these twelve men going to process this new miracle – individually, yet all together at once? Was the fear they felt legitimate or imagined? How would you handle this seemingly paranormal experience? Would you sink to your knees, cower in fright, and yell out as they did?

Then there is Peter. He stepped onto the water in faith, but he soon was overcome by fear. Jesus reached out to save him from drowning. That closeness was evidenced many times in His ministry on Earth with Peter and the other disciples. He was near enough to grab Peter's hand and walk him into the boat. Jesus' timing was perfect. That's no surprise, however, because He invented time at the beginning of Creation.

There was water everywhere, and Peter was about to get a big dose of it. Yet, he was saved by Jesus. That night he experienced a physical salvation. Sometime later, after the resurrection, Jesus went to the Sea of Galilee and found Peter, James, John, Nathanael, Thomas and two other disciples fishing.

Instead of changing the world, they had returned to what they knew best. Jesus cooked them breakfast there on the shore and reconciled Peter to Himself. Spiritual salvation happened with him and the other disciples when Jesus met them in the Upper Room after His resurrection. John's Gospel talks about the Holy Spirit breathed on them by Jesus Himself.

Breakfast on the beach beside the water had a more personal implication, especially for Peter. He had trusted but failed. He had believed but relapsed. He had seen but then forgot. He had found his Savior but had lost himself.

That "me time" with Jesus was his spiritual restitution. Disbelief and disobedience would finally become obedient belief.

Chapter Four - The Doubtful Dozen

One necessary part of the story is to identify the characters involved in the event that night. Jesus had recruited a group of men from different backgrounds to come together into one cohesive unit. But in the case of these very unique individuals, they were more different than the same. And yet they all followed Him. Their distinctive differences made them perfect for the job at hand—all varied but all committed to the same cause.

Here's a brief synopsis of their names, from Matthew Chapter 10: "Now the names of the twelve apostles are these: The first, Simon, who is called Peter, and Andrew his brother; and James the son of Zebedee, and John his brother; Philip and Bartholomew; Thomas and Matthew the tax collector; James the son of Alphaeus, and Thaddaeus;" As well, there was Nathanael and Judas rounding out the dozen.

Although the narrative does not name each of the passengers by name, it would be relatively safe to assume they were all present on that windy voyage. Who were these men, and why were they blindly following an itinerant rabbi whose ancestry was at the time questionable at best? Most of them were uneducated, and they were all not well liked by the general public. How do men who have no real importance in life with no social standing become leaders in a new faith?

In 1967, the box office smash success movie "The Dirty Dozen" starring Lee Marvin and a well-known cast of supporting actors won rave reviews and an Oscar for Best Sound Editing. The story was based on a real life team of soldiers in the 101st Airborne Division during World War II who were known for their bravery through behind the scenes demolition work against the German Third Reich. They were tough. The movie portrayed them in an even more misfit role, with sartorial license. They followed a leader who got the job done.

Contrary to the exploits popularized by Hollywood, the twelve men who followed Jesus were not commissioned to destroy and demoralize the population. Their obedience was the complete opposite. They may have been dirty, but the disciples were commissioned to deliver and develop those around them. Instead of destruction, these men were called to disciple. But first, just like the men in the movie, they had to be trained. Peter and the others found that following Jesus would be the boot camp that would provide them the expertise one day to help people find God.

One of them was a tax collector, who was hated by his peers for selling out his nation to the Roman government, and undoubtedly was on the take under the table. Matthew had a very lucrative and personally profitable career collecting the hardearned income of his fellow Jews.

No wonder he had cause for concern if this spiritual venture collapsed. Not only had he walked away from good money, but the people who knew him hated him for what he was doing to them. But later on, after his time with Jesus, Matthew penned an entire gospel message about those three and a half years. And his words were and are credible to this day.

Not to be outdone, four men made their living by harvesting the bounty of the sea. Some days better than others. At various times during their experience at the book end of their time with the Messiah, they toiled in vain to see any success. If you're a fisherman, and you aren't catching fish, you have a big problem—especially if you earn your livelihood by doing it. Peter, Andrew, brothers James and John (the sons of Zebedee) were familiar with nets, boats, fish, water, and hard work. They were common men doing common labor.

The rest of the crew had no job description to our knowledge, but they definitely had very distinct personalities. Interestingly, they mostly all came from the area around the Sea of Galilee. The four fishermen, plus Matthew and Andrew, came from Bethsaida. Bartholomew, also known as Nathanael, was from Cana where Jesus performed His first miracle. John initially lived in Jerusalem but later moved to Ephesus. Simon the Zealot, Jude, James the Less, and Thomas were from Galilee.

However, there was one who was to be the odd man out—a liar, a thief, and a traitor. Judas Iscariot was from Judea, and he was the one who would constantly be worried about money in spite of the fact that the group entrusted him to take care of their common purse during their years with the One who is called the Christ. At the end of Jesus' earthly ministry, after enduring many hardships and inconveniences over 42 months, Judas would be the lone sellout to the One who promised him eternal life. But Judas never took the offer. His ending is the most tragic of all of these men.

All of these travelers who were called Jesus' disciples were afraid of almost everything. Even Peter, braggadocios, brash, and bold, would wither in times of trouble. He was fearful of not being included, or FOMO (fear of missing out).

He was afraid of drowning in spite of miraculous release from physical limitations. He felt greatly embarrassed by his familiarity and friendship with Jesus during the arrest and trial, genuinely cautious to the point of swearing his innocence of his connection with the man. Peter—loud and proud—was not a leader when he needed to be. However, after the Resurrection, his life took a radical change.

All together these dozen men, average at best, were about to begin a journey with someone who would change their lives forever. The Gospels talk about them, their adventures and travels, their failures and successes, and their relationship not only with each other but with Jesus. He chose each of them for a specific reason, and only He knew why. When each of the twelve were asked about what they wanted, it was almost comical.

Little did any of them know what was to happen to them, or where they would end up. Not one of them really knew what to expect from day to day. All each man knew was that there was something unique about a man called Jesus, and they wanted to know more. The disciples were headed into the great spiritual unknown, and a boat ride in the middle of the night during a tempestuous route on the open water would cause them each to wonder more intently what miracles lay ahead of them.

Did they understand what would happen? No. Were they afraid? Yes. Did they give up and run away after the end of their trip across the Galilee? No. Normal thinking individuals when confronted with incredible situations that are unbelievable have serious questions concerning what they had just experienced. But these men were at once amazed and confused. Each man in that small craft felt that they had just been through a life threatening and traumatic situation, but they saw Jesus show up and save them from near death.

Where did He come from, and how did He get there? For the most part, that really didn't matter after the fact. What did make a difference was that the disciples witnessed an event that no one else had, and they survived it. They were able to talk about it with each other, and later write about it for all the world to live out the same drama through their words.

Was this a time when their faith was tested? Yes, but it was only one of many situations they would encounter during their days with the Savior. The key is that it was only after Jesus rose from the dead that they would begin to understand each of their experiences, including a bad night on the water.

The next twelve chapters talk about each man who served with Jesus. What were they like, and where did they go, not only during their travels with Jesus but also after His ascension to Heaven 40 days after God raised Him from his death. All but one of the twelve had a positive influence on the world. Judas Iscariot did not. The scriptures are very clear about his outcome, including a grisly death that came about by his own hand.

Jesus had significant patience with each of these men as they followed him over the Judean hillsides, by the seashore and onto the water, and through the various towns of the area.

Occasionally, He would call them out because of their disbelief or arrogance, and He would often challenge them to be more than what they were. However, His dealings with these twelve would create in each one a desire to serve Him and others. Early in their time together, this motley little band would argue, disagree, doubt, be clueless, and afraid.

These twelve men were spiritual pygmies. Jesus would enable them to be spiritual giants.

By the time Jesus was arrested, crucified and buried they were slightly better as individuals. Yet, they still only had a small indication as to what He had been teaching them for the previous three and a half years. Talk about dense! Was it due to the culture of the time, or their own belief systems that they had known since childhood? Why were they unable to comprehend what Jesus was saying and doing in spite of hearing and seeing Him 24/7 firsthand? How could unlearned men understand unbelievable physical and spiritual occurrences?

Difficult questions indeed. What answers are best to explain the unexplainable? The intersection of faith and belief has been a challenge for thousands of years. When the disciples stepped into their boat for a supposed brief trip across the Sea of Galilee that night, they were about to enter a teachable moment that took a lifetime to unfold.

Experiential learning is the best kind of education.

This band of twelve would soon learn how to trust, but they would take a much longer time to believe. Their limited faith would be tested. Would they pass or fail? The outcome of the story is telling and is a testament to how faith is put to the test.

Why did Jesus choose each of these men, and why only just twelve? The Bible records that Jesus eventually had many more by the end of his ministry. However, these twelve would be his closest allies and followers. According to the Old Testament, Israel had twelve tribes. Jesus mirrored that number when He chose twelve disciples to represent a new covenant between His Father and His children.

They would be with Him as he wandered the Judean countryside and towns teaching, preaching, healing, and casting out demons. He wanted them to see Him in action. The disciples would learn and go out doing the same thing themselves. They would watch Jesus, listen to Jesus, and mimic much of what he said and did.

And, they were empowered by Him to accomplish those tasks. Only when they doubted did they experience failure and not success. These twelve men were continually learning, and their faith was challenged on a regular basis. Only through their relationship with the Messiah were they ever able to grow.

He didn't need a huge force to accomplish His will. Jesus hand selected personalities that would eventually grow together in unity and then have a common cohesive message to evangelize the known world.

His mission was to usher in the Kingdom of God. Jesus needed men who would become like Him, patterning their lives after the Christ. He knew them long before they knew Him. He knew each man would respond immediately and without hesitation to His clarion call. Over three years later, all but one would continue that work.

The twelve disciples were ordinary men. God used them an extraordinary manner, both as a group and as individuals. Among the twelve were fishermen, a tax collector, and a revolutionary or zealot. Matthew, Mark, Luke and John record their constant failings, their struggles, their fears and their doubts. Witnessing Jesus' resurrection and ascension dramatically changed them. God's Holy Spirit transformed these doubtful dozen into powerful men of God who truly turned the world upside down.

What was the change? Luke indicated that difference in chapter four of his Book of the Acts of the Apostles. Everyone who knew them were amazed about their transformation. The twelve were unschooled. They were ordinary by that day's standards. No scholars were they.

These disciples had "been with Jesus."

Chapter Five -- Andrew

Andrew, the brother of Simon Peter, became the first one called to discipleship according to Greek Orthodoxy. He had a Greek name which means "manly", "brave", or a "man of valor." Either way, to have a non-Jewish name in those days was indicative of a family that was open to cultural differences. There is no recorded Hebrew name for him. Born some time between 5-10 A.D in Bethsaida, he grew up in Galilee and became a fisherman like his brother. He later died in Greece in the town of Patras, part of the then Roman Empire.

As an apostle of Jesus, Andrew enjoyed a definite notoriety, especially after the resurrection and ascension. Commanded by Christ to go and preach the gospel to all parts of the world, Andrew did just that as his mission to his share of the uttermost parts of the earth. Many traditions have developed about the life and death of Andrew after his time with Jesus, primarily because there was not a lot about him in the Gospels, and he played a minor role according to some scholars.

He was the first to be called by Jesus, and the first to claim that Jesus was the Messiah. Although he is mentioned a dozen or less times in the Gospels, Andrew had a sense of closeness with Jesus that some of the others did not enjoy.

He was always referred to in the Scriptures as Peter's brother. Oddly enough, though, it was never the reverse. In other words, Peter was never called Andrew's brother. Perhaps that was because he may have been younger, or that he was less important than Peter, or the writers of the New Testament stories of Jesus felt that's where Andrew ranked in the overall scheme of the disciples.

In theological terms, Andrew is known as the protocletus, meaning "the first called." In Christian cultures, that moniker is a big deal. Someone had to be first, and Andrew was it. Imagine being the first one ever in a brand new faith that would eventually grow into the largest denomination in the world.

His father was named Jonah, which meant Andrew would have had bar-Jonah as a surname, like his brother Simon bar-Jonah. Bar means "son of." Interestingly, the fact that their father named Simon an Aramaic name and Andrew a Greek name reflected the mixed Jewish-Gentile environment around the area of Galilee.

Andrew would possibly have been in his mid-twenties when he started following Jesus. He was able to leave all behind possibly because he was not married at the time. He was in the family fishing business with Peter. However, whenever any boats were mentioned, they were always referenced as belonging not to Andrew but to Peter. They did work together, yet Andrew apparently was the minor partner in their trade. He may have worked for his brother, but he likely didn't have a financial stake.

In the Synoptic Gospels (Matthew, Mark, and Luke), Peter and Andrew—whose Greek name means "manly"—were called from their fishing by Jesus to follow him. Regardless, Andrew was aware of the life of Galilean fishermen, and he knew some of the others that Jesus called. Apparently, he was also a follower of John the Baptist. The apostle John who wrote one of the Gospel accounts mentioned how Andrew became part of the Twelve. He heard the desert evangelist proclaim that Jesus was not only the "Lamb of God,' but also "God's Chosen One."

"The next day John was there again with two of his disciples. When he saw Jesus passing by, he said, "Look, the Lamb of God!"

When the two disciples heard him say this, they followed Jesus. Turning around, Jesus saw them following and asked, "What do you want?" They said, "Rabbi" (which means "Teacher"), "where are you staying?" "Come," he replied, "and you will see." So they went and saw where he was staying, and they spent that day with him. It was about four in the afternoon.

Andrew, Simon Peter's brother, was one of the two who heard what John had said and who had followed Jesus. The first thing Andrew did was to find his brother Simon and tell him, "We have found the Messiah" (that is, the Christ). And he brought him to Jesus." — John 1:35-42.

Andrew knew there was something special about Jesus. He was really the first missionary in his home town. Without recognizing his role, Andrew spoke truth about the One he recognized as the Messiah. He knew it. That character trait eventually grew into his apostolic mission after the ascension of Jesus to Heaven.

Early on, Andrew was respected among the disciples. Andrew and Peter already knew who Jesus was, based on their contact with Him that John wrote about in his gospel. When He officially calls them to be disciples, they respond in a positive manner. In leaving behind the family business, Andrew set a prime example for anyone who would follow Christ.

Believers are instructed to not let anything get in the way of following Jesus' call.

When Jesus told Andrew and Peter they would be "fishers of men," He promised that He would use them to bring men and women to Him for salvation. And that's exactly what Andrew and the other disciples did. He set the pace early on in his relationship with Jesus.

Whenever Andrew is named, it is nearly always in a story about bringing somebody into a relationship with Christ, just as he did with Simon Peter. This character trait has given Andrew an important place in Church memory. Andrew is venerated as a primary example of evangelism in many denominations.

Andrew played a valuable role just the previous day during the miracle on the hillside when Jesus asked for food to feed the 5,000 who had come to hear him preach. They all had been there most of the day and were tired and hungry. When Philip was complaining about not having enough money to buy food, it was Andrew who found the boy with the sack lunch. He was the one who brought the young Jewish child to Jesus.

All of the Gospels record the feeding of the 5,000. However, only John specifically mentions Andrew's role. Jesus instructed the disciples to find food for the thousands who had assembled, and here's Andrew's shining moment:

"When Jesus looked up and saw a great crowd coming toward him, he said to Philip, 'Where shall we buy bread for these people to eat?' He asked this only to test him, for he already had in mind what he was going to do.

Philip answered him, 'It would take more than half a year's wages to buy enough bread for each one to have a bite!'

Another of his disciples, Andrew, Simon Peter's brother, spoke up, 'Here is a boy with five small barley loaves and two small fish, but how far will they go among so many?'"

Once again, Andrew was bringing someone to Jesus. It seemed that he was predestined to continue this role for the rest of his life. Yet, he had a lot more to learn from the Master, and over the proceeding months leading up to the crucifixion, Andrew would indeed get personalized instruction in many more life lessons from Jesus, including the night on the water right after the sack lunch miracle.

Indeed, he was on the water during the windstorm, rowing along with his counterparts. Since Andrew was present at the miracle Jesus had performed by feeding thousands of people with the food that Andrew brought to Him, it is safe to assume he was part of the boat crew later going across the Sea of Galilee. The boat was undoubtedly swaying left to right and pitching up and down. Andrew and his friends had to muster as much strength as they could hour after hour to keep the boat afloat. At one point before Jesus arrived, the boat was rocking at a fever pitch, and they feared for their lives.

The dead of night was no time to be on the lake. Andrew, in spite of his love for Jesus, no doubt was re-thinking this relationship. Then to see out of the mist an apparent ghostlike figure approaching him further exacerbated his sweat and his tears, and perhaps even the possible blood that may have been on his hands from seemingly endless hours of using the oars. Superstition overtook common sense. Faith melted away. Fear gripped his mind and soul. Doomed. Death was sure to follow, he imagined.

Jesus already knew his fear, and the disbelief of the rest of them. He was aware of their plight, yet he wanted them to struggle. Jesus was in a teaching mode that night, as He always was whenever He dealt with anyone. Andrew was no exception. Regardless of his closeness to this Rabbi, Andrew had some growing up to do, and in a hurry. An education of this type was experiential at its highest level.

Knowing how to react in a situation when your life is on the line does not provide a limitless amount of time or guesswork. You must know what to do based on your knowledge, past experiences, and your faith. The ability to synchronize those fundamental elements all at once comes from wisdom – having them is one thing, but how to use them is the key.

Seeking wisdom is best done over a lifetime on an ongoing basis, but you can certainly ask God to provide it when it is needed the most.

Belief in the supernatural was a giant leap for Andrew, as it was for all the others in the boat that night. This single life changing experience immediately elevated Jesus' stature in their eyes. Andrew was not exactly sure how to process what he had just seen, other than to conclude that Jesus had some close affinity with Jehovah.

How close was still subject to further discovery and explanation. Yes, Jesus was special – the Son of God as they all proclaimed; but was that a manifestation of their fear, or a sudden realization that He was Holy, and not just a holy man. There was more to learn.

Andrew early on gained a reputation for expanding his Master's message to people outside the realm of Jewish faith. The Gospel of John recorded an incident when some Greeks had some questions for Jesus. Normally, no self-respecting son of Abraham would be caught dealing with Gentiles as they were considered ceremonially unclean. Jews typically loathed anyone who was not of the same faith or heritage. Judaism was both physical and religious.

Philip, one of Andrew's associates, was approached by the Greeks who sought an audience with Jesus, and he told Andrew about their request. Together, they took the matter to the Messiah for further discussion. When he brought the Greeks to Jesus, Andrew had faith that Jesus' intention was that all men be saved.

He was right. Andrew was an early adopter of an evangelical effort that extended beyond the nation of Israel. The incident with the curious Greeks anticipated the day when Peter, Andrew's brother, would experience God's revelation that all people are welcome to come to Jesus.

Church tradition says that Andrew became an evangelist proclaiming Christ to others in the Greek world. From what is known from church history and tradition, Andrew kept bringing people to Christ, even after Jesus' death. He never seemed to care about putting his own life at risk. It is believed that he was martyred by crucifixion in the city of Patras which was on the northern coast of Peloponnese which was in Greece.

Given the fact that he was likely crucified there, he must have, like many of the other apostles, went well beyond Judea to bring the gospel into all the world from the Great Commission by Jesus. Church historian Eusebius, the 4th century Bishop of Caesarea, wrote that Andrew may have proclaimed the gospel to as far away as Kiev which is now part of Ukraine.

It's interesting that he was crucified like Christ but in the pattern or shape of an "X" which was often a Christian symbol. Because of that design, he also became the patron saint of Scotland in later centuries.

Andrew, like his brother Peter, considered himself unworthy of being crucified in the same manner as Christ was, and therefore, his execution was on what has historically been named St. Andrew's cross. He was crucified around 70 AD. Andrew gave the ultimate sacrifice for Jesus.

Peter, his brother, traveled from Jerusalem through Antioch and reached Rome to exercise his universal mission of preaching Christ crucified, and then became alive again for the forgiveness of sin; Andrew, instead, was the Apostle of the Greek world and took his role as the missionary to the Hellenistic environs and its people.

So it is that in life and in death they appear as respective true brothers with what today are the Roman Catholic and Greek Orthodox denominations. These men became martyrs for the cause of Christ and the sake of the gospel. Two millennia after they lived and died, their spiritual legacies are alive around the world. Were they alive today, each man would still be pointing to Jesus as the Way, the Truth and the Life.

Chapter Six – Jude, Son of James

Jude, the son of James. He is clearly distinguished separately from Judas Iscariot, another apostle and later the betrayer of Jesus Christ. Both Jude and Judas are translations of the name in the same Koine Greek original text of the New Testament, which in turn is a Greek variant of Judah, a name which was common among Jews at the time. Judas was a popular name in New Testament times. It means, "Jehovah leads."

Bible scholars suggest that Judas was likely the name given to Thaddeus at birth   while Lebbaeus and Thaddeus were nicknames. Those names all identified the same individual. Interestingly, Catholics and Protestants differ on exactly Jude's relationship with Jesus. The former denomination holds to their belief that he was His brother, and the latter disagree on this relationship. Scholars in both camps feel that they have the right interpretation of the name from their respective Biblical texts.

In some New Testament passages, the name Thaddaeus appears among the list of twelve Apostles. But in other New Testament passages, the name Judas (son of James) appears instead. In ancient times, a person could have two or three different names, such as a Greek-language name and a Hebrew name. Additionally, at times people were known primarily by their occupational title.

He is generally identified by the following names: Thaddeus, Jude, Jude Thaddaeus, Judas Thaddaeus, or Lebbaeus. Matthew's gospel in the King James version of the Bible identifies him this way *"Labbaeus, whose surname was Thaddaeus."* The name Lebbaeus translates as "breast child, or child of one's heart, or man of heart." Some scholars believe he is the author of the Jude's epistle. Yet, others disagree with this opinion.

The name Thaddaeus appears in the list of Apostles given in Matthew 10:3, between James, son of Alphaeus, and Simon the Zealot. In Mark 3:18, the name Thaddaeus appears, again, in the same placement. In Acts 1:13, however, a man named Judas (son of James) is listed below Simon.

In Luke 6:16, Judas (son of James), is listed again among the group of twelve disciples who were called by Jesus, between Simon the Zealot and Judas Iscariot. The two names - Judas (son of James) and Thaddaeus - never appear in the same book, lending credibility to the belief by many Bible scholars that the names both refer to the same person.

If you cross-reference the four Gospels, most scholars have agreed that the Thaddaeus in the books of Matthew and Mark is the same person as Judas in the books of Luke and John. Matthew also refers to this disciple as Lebbaeus and Judas the Zealot, whereas Luke and the Acts of the Apostles record him as Judas, son of James.

There is very limited information about this disciple. Little is known of the early life of Thaddeus. He was probably born and raised in the same area of Galilee as Jesus and the other disciples. One tradition has him born into a Jewish family in the town of Paneas. Still another tradition says that his mother was a cousin of Mary, mother of Jesus. That relationship would make him a blood relation to Jesus.

Also, there are differing opinions about him being the author of the single chapter Book of Jude in the New Testament. Some scholars believe he was the writer, and others hold to the one who penned it as the half brother of Jesus who was also named Jude, aka Judas.

This viewpoint is one that has been accepted by many evangelical theologians. The history of its origination is hard to date, but the likelihood of the Book of Jude being written shortly after Peter wrote his epistles around 65 A.D. is very strong based on the similarity of the information referenced in the Epistle of Jude.

After Jesus' ascension to Heaven, Judas (Thaddeus), like other disciples, preached the gospel in the years following the death of Jesus. Tradition holds that he proclaimed the gospel in Judea, Samaria, Idumaea, Syria, Mesopotamia, and Libya, possibly with Simon the Zealot. Church tradition holds that Thaddeus founded a church at Edessa and was crucified there as a martyr. One legend suggests his execution occurred in Persia. Because he was executed by an ax or club, these weapons are often shown in artworks depicting Thaddeus.

After his execution, the body of Thaddeus was reported to have been brought to Rome and placed in St. Peter's Basilica. Supposedly his bones remain to this day, interred in the same tomb with the remains of Simon the Zealot. Saint Jude is the patron saint of Armenians. They believe that Thaddeus' remains are buried in an Armenian monastery.

But what about his relationship with the Messiah? John's gospel records that Thaddeus asked Jesus, why he wasn't revealing Himself to the world and only to the disciples. This question uncovered a few things about Thaddeus.

First, Thaddeus was comfortable in his relationship, enough to stop Jesus in the middle of His teaching to ask a question. This disciple was curious about this matter. Second, it demonstrated that Thaddeus was compassionate. He had a heart for the world beyond the Jews. He wanted everyone to know Jesus.

When Thaddeus was in the boat on the Sea of Galilee the night that Jesus appeared to them walking on the water, no doubt he, too, was frightened almost to death. He knew his love for the Christ; but his fear of spirits was greater, until he recognized Jesus as the approaching person destined to show His divine ability to display the miraculous. There is no statement in any of the gospel accounts that Thaddeus made comments, other than to agree in tandem with the rest that Jesus was the Son of God.

Rowing for all he was worth, Thaddeus had suddenly recognized when Jesus showed up that he was in the midst of a miracle in the making. Did he understand it? No. Did he believe it? Yes. Did he wish to know more about the reason behind it? Probably. Miracles don't usually take place every day, or for that matter, every night.

Separating vision from reality is tough to do even in the best of circumstances.

Thaddeus was just trying to get from one place to another like Jesus told him to do. That's all. He probably really didn't want to go out on the Sea of Galilee at night, but he really didn't have much of a choice. He did what he was told. In that sense, he was obedient, but reluctantly so. Later, he would come to know the truth.

During the days that followed, Judas Thaddeus was more than curious, like the rest of the twelve. He wanted to know more about this God-Man, Jesus. He hadn't ever seen anything like what he saw that night, and he hadn't ever met anyone like Him. The Messiah had caused Judas to think about his beliefs and his faith. He required these men to accept Him at face value. Yet when He taught them about Himself, they chose to ignore His most valuable lessons during His life on earth before the crucifixion.

Following the ascension of Jesus to Heaven, Judas is named among the disciples that met together in prayer in Jerusalem waiting on what had been foretold by their teacher. When Pentecost happened, the filling of the Holy Spirit was evident to those in attendance, including Judas Thaddeus. He was listed in the Book of Acts as being present with the others, except for the other Judas who had died after the crucifixion.

Luke, a Greek and a physician by trade, became an apostle after encountering the stories of Jesus. He was a great help to the Apostle Paul, and he became an authority on the life of Jesus and the early spread of Christianity in the Roman Empire. It was Luke who gave such detailed accounts of the Messiah, the disciples and the church in its infancy. He named Judas Thaddeus in his writings as part of those who were closest to Jesus.

There is sufficient, although scant, Biblical text surrounding the existence of Judas Thaddeus and his participation with Jesus. Much of the material is, of course, from the gospels and the Book of Acts. No real extra-Biblical writings talk about Jude other than some historical accounts created by the fourth century Christian scholar Jerome who translated much of the Greek texts into Latin, called the Vulgate. He was responsible for creating the document that was used for one thousand years by the church as the official New Testament.

Jerome called him Thaddaeus Trinomius, which means a man with three names. He is called Thaddeus in Mark's gospel. He also is called Lebbaeus, whose surname was Thaddeus, in Matthew's gospel account. Jude had various names like some of the other disciples. However, this is not surprising. Prior to the crucifixion, there was a need to distinguish him from the other apostle Judas Iscariot, who betrayed Jesus. In those days it was common for men to have three names.

Thaddaeus may well have had Judas as another name. Possibly, when the name Judas became a name of shame, he may have chosen to drop it and be known as Thaddaeus. Another possibility is that Thaddaeus could be the same name as Theudas, which could easily become Judas. As a result the Hebrew name of God would be replaced by the Greek 'theos'.

God honors faithfulness.

Giving proper attribution has been challenging over the past two millennia. Facts become legend, and those become myth. The historicity of men from the early days of the first century is often very sketchy. Church traditions get garbled, morphed, and lost among factual inconsistencies.

What is known is that Jude was a real man who lived at a real time in a real place. He had real relationships with others including the disciples and with Jesus. His life although limited in literal scope was important enough to be recorded in holy scripture and kept alive for two thousand years.

Seven – Wave Walker Two

Simon Peter, the big fisherman, went through an emotional roller coaster on this nighttime boat ride, in addition to other life experiences. Eventually, he ended up penning two letters that became part of the New Testament. Here's the one who decides to be brave, even though he was probably full of fear on that first step. His faith in the One who beckoned him out onto a roiling sea was strong enough to move out of the boat, but not strong enough to keep him from sinking.

Peter was always speaking out, and sometimes that got him into hot water. In this case, his rash desire to prove his faith put him in the forefront of the story and landed him directly on the water. Matthew wrote that it was Peter who decided to join their Master, and no one else. Peter was the one who wanted to be large and in charge with this group. His bigger than life personality was bold and brash – all the time.

Peter was the boldest of all the disciples, and that made him unique. He would say things that others would only think. He was that one guy who acted when others did not have the nerve to move. Peter wanted to follow Jesus with his entire being. His heart was completely drawn to Jesus. However, this loud Galilean was full of mistakes, and he would pay for them many times over throughout his life.

His life is rich with experience and influence. It was also full of contradictions. He was part of Jesus' inner circle, but he was also called out by Him as Satan when Peter once spoke out of turn. Christ longed to be spiritually intimate with Peter and with the other disciples.

By choosing them to follow Him, He was able to pour Himself into their lives day after day during the time they spent together. Peter longed for a mighty faith, but he fell down often. Jesus turned an illiterate, rough and tough fisherman into the leader of the Christian faith. If He could do that for Peter, Jesus can accomplish the same in you.

Who was Peter, and why has he been held up as the epitome of discipleship and faith, revered by Christians for two thousand years? His life story is one of the greatest told in history about redemption. Fishermen usually were known for being vulgar and hot tempered. Usually, they were uneducated and brash. They were often stereotyped as sometimes violent, very active and physical, and not afraid of other people.

Peter, like all other men, was sinful. When Jesus found him, he would move from his fishing job to a ministry position. Yet, his personality would not immediately change. Over time, after living with the Messiah for over three years, he would become a leader in the Christian church after Pentecost. But that would happen only after years of deeply personal interaction with the Son of God, especially including his nighttime experience on the Sea of Galilee.

Peter like the others in the boat were deathly afraid of spirits. A common superstition among seafarers of the day in ancient times was those who drowned would haunt the waters. When Peter saw Jesus coming to the crew in the middle of the night, he certainly wasn't expecting this approaching phantom-like creature to be the Messiah. Fear was rampant, and faith came slowly after Jesus called out to identify Himself.

Was this big, brave Galilean taunting this mysterious wave walker as a sign of his bravado, or was he truly, legitimately asking and hoping for the truth? He was known for being somewhat headstrong. Peter was quick to speak before he thought things through. He was impetuous. While that got him occasionally into trouble, it also prompted Peter to experience things no one else did.

Peter was willing to put it all on the line that night. He wanted to exhibit his courage to Jesus in spite of his fear and the unknown. Along with the other disciples, Peter had been straining against the waves and wind all night long when Jesus appeared to them, walking on the water. He was full of courage and confidence, willing to literally step onto the roiling waters because He was looking right at Jesus. Initially it went well for a few minutes, until Peter started to sink. He had taken his eyes off the One who kept him safe.

Why did Jesus invite Peter to come out to Him and not any of the other disciples? Because Peter asked. He is the only one of the twelve who requested to step out of the boat. Knowing Peter, it's not surprising he would want to take on this task. The others may have wanted to jump out of the boat and walk to Jesus, but none of them dared to even say a word. Peter asked Jesus to let him come to Him. He waited for Jesus to call him. Then Peter obeyed.

In the dark of the night, as winds were hurling the boat around and around and whipping up the waves into a frothy frenzy, Peter showed enough faith to step out of a semi-dry boat onto the lake's surface. Initially, his eyes were transfixed on Jesus' face. He seemed at first unconcerned about his immediate environment. He felt at that moment in time that Jesus would prevent him from sinking.

His faith was strong as long as Peter was focused on his spirit man. He was now fully aware of the power Jesus held over nature. Also, Peter knew Jesus loved him, and that Jesus would not fail him.

Let's stop for just a brief moment and look at what was happening. What lesson can be applied to this situation? How do Christians make sense of the storms of life surrounding them, and how do you know what to do when life buffets you like tornadic winds? The answer is really simple.

Faith is strengthened as long as your focus is on Jesus.

He has power over all things. There is nothing He cannot do because He is God. Jesus loves you with an unconditional love — enough to give His life for you.

As a Believer, you understand that He is completely deserving of your love and your trust in Him. Keeping your focus on Jesus throughout life's storms provides an opportunity for your faith to grow. He never promised that His followers would not face challenges or difficulties. He only said He would be with you through both good and bad times.

Matthew's words provide a great picture. Peter started to doubt which caused him literally to be shaken in the storm. He was being tossed about by the water and the wind. Peter began to sink. Was it because Jesus suddenly lost His supernatural power to hold up Peter, or that nature was stronger than the One who created it? No. What did change, though? It was the disciple. Peter began to doubt as he removed his gaze away from the Christ.

Peter began to look at the situation, not the Savior. He was overwhelmed by the circumstances. His viewpoint was shattered once he stopped looking at the One who was saving Him. All of a sudden, Peter felt that the things around him were more powerful than Jesus. What he forgot was that while his attention was on Jesus, his situation on the waves was not a threat to him. His comfort zone became uncomfortable due to his actions and his disobedience. It was his fault that he started to sink. Jesus was right there the entire time.

What is another lesson to be learned from Peter's experience? Faith is removed when fear reigns in your life. But fear has no power or place when faith is reigning in you. Like oil and water, fear and faith do not mix. Unfortunately for Peter, his fear overcame his faith. He forgot at that moment who Jesus was, and his boldness became unbelief. When Jesus reached out to Peter, it was a life saving manifestation of Jesus' divine nature. Peter undoubtedly had no other recourse than to believe, even though his faith had been shattered by his own disobedience and lack of trust.

Jesus did not refer to Peter's "little faith" because He required evidence to force him to believe. Jesus does not demand blind faith. He never has and never will. The definition of faith is not believing in something without evidence. Faith is putting trust in someone who is trustworthy. Jesus fulfilled that during His ministry, living out His life daily in front of the men He asked to follow Him, and in front of thousands of others over His life on Earth.

The Greek word Jesus used with Peter about his faith being small translates to small or puny conviction. More simply put, Peter's confidence vanished. He lacked the ability to trust or believe once he became afraid of his circumstances. The issue was not about requiring evidence. It was about trust.

Once that disappeared from Peter, he lost hope. What a valuable object lesson. Losing hope leads to losing trust, which in turn results in losing faith. Peter lost all three that night, and it would take time to regain them. He was used as the example of what not to do when you take your eyes off Jesus.

When Peter and Jesus returned into the boat, the disciples as a group had an epiphany. They had just experienced another phenomenal miracle, and it was a big one. They had seen Jesus in His ministry perform other amazing things. Those miracles may have given them pause to wonder about who Jesus was, but now they were finally understanding more about Him. When they saw that Peter would be used by Jesus to walk on water, it changed their lives.

Many of the twelve had known Peter his entire life. They knew him and how he could be just a plain, outspoken fisherman that was uneducated and full of brash behavior. This time, however, was different. Peter trusted Jesus to help him with an impossible feat. To actually walk on water without any help or support was truly miraculous. Not only that, but Jesus made the wind and water calm down as soon as the two of them stepped out of the lake and into the boat. Who could do such things?

Yet the story told by Matthew does not really focus on the miracle itself. Jesus walking on water was only an outward manifestation of what happened at the climax of the story. In spite of the miracles they had seen within the previous twenty four hours, it wasn't about those. The key to the passage is all about the disciples worshiping Jesus. It is the first time they address Jesus as the Son of God, and finally they were just beginning to learn who Jesus claimed to be.

Peter was transformed himself from a lowly common Galilean into a leader among men. But something even greater had happened that night. Now the disciples recognized Jesus as the Son of God. Walking on waves for Peter would be a memory he would keep forever. He would not repeat it, nor would he ask for it to be repeated. There became more important needs in his life as the ministry with Jesus would continue.

Jesus would chastise Peter for losing his faith on the waves that night. He would let Peter know that it was not the storm that was causing him to lose his trust in Jesus. Peter would learn more about losing faith toward the end of his journey with Jesus before the crucifixion. He would also find the strength to regain it. Ironically, both lessons were learned by the Sea of Galilee. Peter learned life the hard way. That was his way.

Jesus asks you from time to time to step out of your comfort zone. Remember, the storm was still going on when Peter was encouraged to step out of the boat. It wasn't until after he was saved from drowning and then climbed back into the boat with Jesus holding him up did the winds and waves go still. He may ask you to take a risk to trust Him. Sometimes, you have to step out of the boat to strengthen your faith.

Complacency and comfort are generally the rule for most Believers. When storms come, faith gets put to the test. Are you going to sink or stand during your storm? Perhaps the most important life lesson from Matthew's account of Peter walking on water is the response to the power of Jesus.

Worshiping Him is more important than the event itself.

Jesus commands worship when you encounter Him. That is the whole point of this story in Matthew's gospel. It really was not about Peter, his lack of faith, or the disciples fearing the storm and its consequences or even fear of Jesus appearing to them at night on the open sea. Ultimately, the truth focuses on the power of Jesus, who He is, and your response to Him.

As a Believer, you should have the same response to Jesus as the disciples. Be reminded of His character, His position, His divinity, His faithfulness, and His ability to save and rescue you. Dwell in Him for worship. Like Peter and the other eleven men found out, peace is not found in the absence of turmoil, fear and uncertainty, but in the presence of Jesus.

Peter never realized when he decided to follow this itinerant rabbi that his life would be turned upside down, not only during his living years, but also literally at his death. Peter took risks. He didn't play it safe. His existence with Jesus was nothing but excitement.

He had tough times, but he overcame them through the power of his faith in Christ. He went through incredible highs and lows, yet he survived to tell the story of the life of Jesus and the good news of His resurrection. Peter experienced the power that was promised to him by the Messiah. He testified about it over and over until his execution years later by the Roman Government.

Peter's story is every Believer's story.

His journey is the same for everyone who experiences both success and failure as a Christian. He started out strong, but often got in his own way. He made huge mistakes. He wanted to do the right thing, but he would fail miserably at some very critical life moments. He demanded attention by his very nature, but he would shrink in the night when it mattered the most.

He abandoned his faith walk by the shore of Galilee, but he resumed it there again when Jesus restored him. Peter's faith was renewed, but at a cost. It was the price he paid for disobedience, doubt and fear.

There is no doubt that Peter remembered the major highlights of his life with Jesus, and he would play them over and over in his mind as he ministered in the life of the newly established religion called "the Way."

He would be reminded about the times he was a hero, but more often he would be mindful of the times he was not. For one shining minute, he defied gravity and nature. He walked on water. He was out in front of the rest of the disciples. He would know the joy of victorious living, but also the humility of tragic decisions. Believers today, like Peter of old, can experience both victory and defeat based on their level of faith in Jesus.

God wants you to experience "Wave Walker" moments in your life.

He wants to write a great story with you as the primary character. His faithfulness can provide multiple faith filled experiences as you seek to learn more about worship, obedience, service, trust and faith. Too often, Christians seek to be safe and comfortable. Those are good options, but a life lived as a disciple is not one typically reserved for lukewarm living. Faith should be active and richly fulfilling. God seeks to do things in you and through you that you cannot even imagine.

Peter matured in his faith as a result of his life with Jesus, and he lived another three decades after the Ascension telling people about the Messiah. This man called Jesus was the One who was sent to redeem mankind from sin. Peter repeated this Gospel message for thirty years to multiplied thousands of both Jews and Gentiles. His faith continued to expand with unbelievable results, recorded in the New Testament for Believers to read and accept as a testimony of forgiveness and faith.

Uneducated, nonetheless Peter preached with boldness during his ministry. Once fearful, he became emboldened in his faith. This disciple performed many miracles including bringing the dead back to life as recorded in Luke's story of the Acts of the Apostles.

He traveled the region and shared Jesus' message of forgiveness, faith and salvation. He endured many persecutions. He was frequently imprisoned. He ultimately suffered death by execution, as church tradition holds, being crucified upside down. He felt unworthy to die as Jesus had.

God used Peter to reach his world. His life was a fulfillment of grace and mercy. Peter endured until the end. His life counted then, and it counts now as one who was sold out to Jesus for the mission of spreading the gospel.

The story of his redemption has lifted untold millions of souls out of dull and boring lives to count for a cause greater than themselves. His role as a Wave Walker began a chain reaction in the lives of the disciples that still resonates two thousand years after it happened. It's ripple effect on eternity is doubtless beyond the scope of knowledge and imagination.

As a modern day disciple, are you keeping your focus on Jesus? Losing your focus on Him has damaging short and long term effects on so many aspects of life. By taking your eyes off Jesus weakens your faith. You may believe in Him, but your faith as a Believer falls into a state of limited affect. Your marriage can suffer due to a damaged relationship with your spouse.

Your career may collapse because you have failed to honor God in your business dealings. Your children may be wayward from your lack of keeping your home in a proper Christian environment. You may experience health crises due to a lack of consistent lifestyle choices with your diet or other habits that are not honoring to God. Your thought life may degrade because of what you watch or view.

When Jesus is not the primary source of your spiritual strength, your faith is in trouble. Your ability to weather the storms of life is lessened, and you may find yourself trying to do it all in your own power. Those who do not know Him talk a lot about self-dependence and the power of their will. They concentrate on individual ability.

Unbelievers feel they can accomplish whatever they want through their own talents. In the eyes of the world, all those actions and attitudes make sense. After all, who needs to rely on someone they cannot even see, feel or hear! Unfortunately, they are dead wrong -- initially spiritually, and eventually eternally wrong.

Wouldn't you want to know with certainty that your final destination is not up to you, but to the One who created you? Through the journey make sure that your course is set, your compass is true, and your way is certain.

At the end of life, faith in God through His Son Jesus is what carries you to an eternal reward. Until then, being capable of surviving the storms of life requires reliance on Him.

Chapter Eight - Nathanael

Nathanael, the likely brother of Philip, was also called Bartholomew. His hometown was Cana in the area around Galilee. Although he was chosen to be one of Jesus' original twelve disciples, not much is recorded about him in the Gospels or in the Book of Acts. However, he was the first to recognize who Jesus was. Nathanael has the distinction of being the first recorded person to confess belief in Jesus as the Son of God and Savior.

The name Bartholomew is a family designation, meaning "son of Tolmai," which implies that he had another name. Nathanael means "gift of God" or "giver of God." One encounter noted in the Gospels is with Jesus Christ in which He declared that Nathanael was a model Jew and a man of integrity open to the work of God. Jesus noted that Nathanael was without guile or deceit. Jesus identified Nathanael with Jacob, the father of the Israelite nation.

The Gospel of John describes Nathanael's call by Philip. John's Gospel says that Philip found Nathanael and told him, "We have found the one Moses wrote about in the Law, and about whom the prophets also wrote—Jesus of Nazareth, the son of Joseph." (John 1:45). Imagine getting to meet for the first time the person whom you had been educated about your entire life, and then be able to actually live and work with Him. That concept must have buzzed his brain and his spirit for some time after he met Jesus.

At first, Nathanael was skeptical about the idea of a Messiah from Nazareth. He scoffed at Philip, *"Nazareth! Can anything good come from there?"* (John 1:46). He would have been familiar with Nazareth, which is only 4 miles southwest of Cana. It was well known that a Roman garrison was stationed in Nazareth. The Jewish men who made money doing business with the Roman soldiers were considered traitorous collaborators, while the women who did the same were considered worse.

But Philip encouraged him, *"Come and see."* As they approached Him, Jesus revealed that he had seen Nathanael sitting under a fig tree before Philip called him. Jesus astonished Nathanael, demonstrating supernatural power by referring to Nathanael's experience under the fig tree. How could that happen? Jesus' divinity was evidenced that day.

Jesus' greeting captured Nathanael's attention by His penetrating insight, and it threw him off guard. Nathanael was stunned to learn that Jesus already knew him and that He was aware of his movements. Jesus' personal knowledge of Nathanael and the recent event under the fig tree caused Nathanael to respond with an amazing confession of faith, proclaiming Jesus to be the divine Son of God and King of Israel.

In Jewish thought the idea of sitting under a fig tree was an image of peace and security using word pictures dating back to the peaceful conditions of Solomon's reign. A man could sit under his fig tree, undisturbed and untroubled, praying and meditating upon God's word.

There was something in Jesus's words that had a tremendous impact upon Nathanael, captivating him to want to know more about Jesus. It is not just that the Christ saw him sitting under a fig tree that caused Nathanael to make his bold proclamation about Jesus.

It is very possible that when Nathanael heard Jesus' statement about him that he realized Jesus possessed a clear insight into the thoughts that Nathanael was thinking about under the fig tree. Jesus' intimate knowledge of the thoughts and meditations of Nathanael's heart produced this reaction. Jesus had touched not only his mind but also his emotions and his soul. Nathanael understood that Jesus had seen into the depths of his heart.

Seemingly Nathanael concluded that Jesus must be the Son of God and the King of Israel. By using these titles Nathanael expressed his conviction that Jesus is the Messiah. His faith had been challenged and stirred. This disciple never really had a problem in believing in something and someone good. Believing now had real meaning.

Trusting in Jesus is the beginning. Living for Him is the commitment and challenge. Being like Him is the goal.

Jesus also promised Nathanael that he would see a stunning vision of Him. He then added, "Very truly I tell you, you will see 'heaven open, and the angels of God ascending and descending on' the Son of Man." (John 1:51). Upon meeting Jesus for the first time, Nathanael overcame his initial skepticism about the insignificance of Nazareth and left his past behind. Trust. Commitment. Becoming. Nathanael would experience all of these.

John gives an accurate representation of Nathanael, revealing some important aspects of Nathanael's character–his relationships with other disciples, his honest and sincere personality, and his thoughtful reflection upon God's word. Nathanael was close to Philip, Peter and Andrew.

They were from the same area, in the same trade, and were all Galileans seeking for the Messiah before their encounter with Jesus. Nathanael was searching the Old Testament scriptures for Him, and their mutual interest and friendship led them to follow Jesus. His spiritual interest was the catalyst for Nathanael to leave all he knew behind.

Nathanael would have been in the crowd on that stormy overnight boat trip on the Sea of Galilee. None of the gospels spell out whom all was going out on the lake when Jesus commanded them to sail away to the other side. However, it is safe to assume that because this little cruise happened after the feeding of the 5,000 with the disciples scurrying around distributing fish and bread to the masses, that Nathanael was also part of the rowing crew.

When Jesus climbed aboard the boat with Nathanael and the rest of them, the wind completely dropped to a calm. They gladly took him aboard. But they were each one scared out of their wits. They had not had the sense to learn the lesson of the loaves and fishes. Even that amazing miracle had not opened their eyes to see who Jesus was, as the Bible says that their hearts were hardened.

The final time Nathanael is seen was after Jesus' resurrection, and he didn't have any more questions. There on the shore of the Sea of Galilee, where it all started, he saw the risen Christ, and his faith was confirmed. Seven of the original doubting dozen had reverted back to their original jobs.

They were fishing. Or at least they were trying to fish. Just like the fateful night on the water when the wind was against them, this time the fish were against them. These rough and ready men who made their living by their trade on the lake were floundering in failure.

Then, some stranger on the shore taunts them into trying another option. They were probably thinking, "Who does this landlubber think he is, and who does he think we are?!" But because they were experiencing abysmal results, it wouldn't hurt to try another way. They did not recognize Jesus, and they had no good results to show for their efforts.

When their nets were breaking with so many fish, they relived a moment remembered from another time before. Immediately Nathanael and the rest knew Jesus had come to rescue them once again. The Bible says that nobody dared ask Jesus, "Who are you?" They just knew. The time for questions had passed, and Nathanael's faith was not only confirmed, but it was also restored.

Nathanael's character teaches that a disciple is an honest searcher of the truth.

He is honest about his faith and his doubts, and he is honest about his thoughts and reflections. Honesty and sincerity are character qualities that allow Jesus to trust you as His disciple. These traits also help you develop and maintain relationships with other Believers. As well, a thoughtful, reflective disposition leads to meaningful conversations about important spiritual matters.

Church tradition says Nathanael carried a translation of the Gospel of Matthew to northern India. Legend claims he was crucified upside down in Albania. Nathanael died a martyr's death for Christ. However, like most of the other disciples, Nathanael abandoned Jesus during his trial and crucifixion. But this disciple was redeemed. That's what Jesus does.

The vast majority of individuals who do not believe in Jesus base their beliefs on unqualified impressions. They may have heard people who claim to know the Bible talk about it, but they have never studied the evidence for themselves. They have never taken the time to study the Bible in depth. To them, Philip's invitation to "come and see" Jesus for themselves applies as much today as it did to Nathanael two millennia ago.

Through the story of Nathanael in the Bible, you can see that your personal prejudices can skew your judgment. But by being open to God's word, individuals come to know the truth. Nathanael's story endures as an ideal example of how a true believer responds to Jesus Christ. For him, skepticism turned to belief, which then in turn became faith. The same can happen with you.

Chapter Nine – Taxed Beyond Belief

Matthew was Jewish, but not in practice during his time behind the tax desk. His father Alphaeus had named him Levi. He wrote a key gospel story which was chosen as the first book of the New Testament—the life of Jesus from a Jewish perspective. Matthew knew his audience; and because of his personal relationship with the Carpenter from Nazareth, he knew what elements to include to make it applicable to his people first, then to anyone else who would read it.

The details Matthew would include in his New Testament letter would resonate in his day, and still resonate with current reader two millennia later. Who would believe a ghost story about two men walking on the top of the open Sea of Galilee, one of the most iconic lakes in the world. Yet, most everyone in his day believed in spirits, demons and disembodied souls.

His text would not have been considered unusual as it relates to seeing a spirit of some kind walking at night. What suspicion would have been raised would be largely related to who or what type of spirit or ghost it was. Jesus was approaching them, but He was too far off to be recognized until Peter saw Him. Although there is no definitive language as to the distance from their boat to their nocturnal visitor, it can be logically assumed that the Rabbi was close enough to be recognized in the middle of a huge life-threatening storm.

Similar to Mark's account, Matthew records Jesus giving instructions and the situation as if reporting it for the news. Yet, Matthew is the only one who records the response Peter made to the situation, and their following declaration of the deity of Jesus.

Keeping in mind that his readers were primarily Jews, Matthew was clearly identifying who Jesus was. To the nation of Israel, the Messiah would be a king among men, not a lowly rabbi who kept the company of common people of the day. Matthew endeavored in his account of the gospel to show Jesus not only in his humanity but also in his divine nature.

Matthew was Jewish by birth and was not well respected by others, primarily because he sold himself to the Roman government for the position of a tax collector which the Jews hated.

When Jesus came to his table and said, *"Follow Me,"* Matthew immediately left his income, his position, his business life, and all else to be with the One who owns the cattle who created the universe and owns it all. Did this man who cheated his neighbors know the itinerant preacher who asked him to walk away from everything he knew and trusted?

Not really. The power of Jesus' words was so intense that it didn't matter. Matthew somehow suspected that his old life was over and a new one was about to begin. Somewhere between leaving behind guaranteed income and a life of ease and trying to row a little boat across an angry lake in the middle of the night, Matthew was growing in his faith. Did he understand it? Did he know what to anticipate? Was he afraid of the future? Was he constantly surprised? NO, NO, YES, YES. In that order.

But let's look at what event had just happened that day leading up to their overnight jaunt on the lake. The miraculous feat of Jesus walking on the water, written in three of the four Gospel accounts, came right after His miracle of feeding 5,000 hungry Hebrews with only five loaves of bread and two fish.

However, it was the revelation of Jesus walking on the water that, more than any other, convinced the disciples that He was surely the Son of God. Matthew recorded that when Jesus got into the boat the wind ceased. But first Peter walked on the water at Jesus' command, demonstrating His power as the Word of God.

The divine nature of the Christ allowed Him to supercede the laws of gravity, the laws of physics, the laws of nature, and overrule the

Creation that He established in the Beginning.

When Matthew was in the middle of the situation with the other disciples, he had to know that what he was seeing violated every aspect of natural law. Yet, he knew Jesus was right there in front of him – in the flesh. He could reach out and touch Him physically and talk with Him. He had the ability to remember and record this supernatural event for posterity.

Seeing Jesus walk out of the darkness on top of the Sea of Galilee and watching Him beckon Peter to jump overboard and meet Him on the waves had to have been the most surreal vision he had ever seen. Even beyond what he had just experienced a few hours before with Jesus feeding over 5,000 people with a little boy's lunch.

By now in his time with the Messiah, Matthew had obviously witnessed some unusual circumstances, but this one was the most dynamic scenario to date. Because Matthew was used to financial transactions as a tax collector, he understood basic math. He knew that one plus one makes two. He knew weights and measures.

His job before meeting the Christ face to face was being able to make sense of physical transactions. Although he was not a scientist, Matthew had full understanding that no one can walk on water because of the physical nature of water and weight. So, how could this have happened?

Who was this Jesus?

At the initial sighting of what they thought was a paranormal being, this ghost became more real each moment he came closer to their boat. With the wind as strong as it was through the night, and with the intense physicality of their struggle to row toward the opposite shore for hours on end without progress, Matthew had to have been mentally struggling with the fact that this creature of some sort was gaining on them and not being encumbered by the same wind they were fighting. How could this be happening?

When did Matthew recognize Jesus? The ethereal nature of how the scene was unfolding likely made him very uncomfortable, and he probably feared for his life. As a Jew, he would have heard the stories from his days as a youth in the temple when the rabbi would be reminding the congregation not to be involved in any demonic spiritual activity.

He had been educated about the story with King Saul consorting with a witch and summoning back the dead, which was direct disobedience against God's commands. Matthew surely was not willing to fall away from God by interacting with ghosts or evil spirits.

When Jesus was close enough to the boat and was able to hear Him talk with Peter, Matthew must have at least heard some of the conversation as it was taking place. Did he realize what was about to happen? This disciple must have suspected that Peter was putting his life at risk by deciding to exit their watercraft and hold hands with their leader. Did Matthew hear Jesus tell them not to be afraid, or was the wind so strong that it overpowered His voice.

When the God of the Universe speaks in the midst of a tempestuous situation, most people hear Him.

Matthew wrote in detail about the exact works Jesus spoke. He was able to remember and write down the calming sentences that came from his Master's mouth. "It is I. Don't fear." And Peter had the audacity to question Jesus' veracity. Truth was being spoken, and the most outspoken of the bunch dared to call for proof. Talk about boldness!

Matthew knew that Peter would probably be the only one to speak a dare, almost tempting Jesus to prove Himself. Where would Peter go if he jumped ship? Was it possible he, too, could defy natural law by stepping onto the Sea of Galilee?

This former taxman provided the nation of Israel an answer to their questions about Jesus. Two thousand years later, his text still resonates with freshness and truthfulness as if the boat ride just happened yesterday. Each time you read this passage of Scripture, the Holy Spirit illuminates your mind as a Believer to another aspect of divine knowledge that provides fresh insight and perspective.

Chapter Ten -- Philip

Philip, one of the Twelve, hailed from Bethsaida which was a small town in the area near Galilee. Jesus confronted him personally to be one of His disciples. How interesting it is that Philip brought Nathanael (also known as Bartholomew) to Jesus. And, Andrew brought Peter to Jesus. No one brought Philip to Jesus. The Gospel of John states that Jesus went to Galilee to recruit followers. He found Philip and spoke only two simple words, *"Follow Me."* Philip did exactly that without hesitation.

There is not a lot of information recorded about Philip, except for a few stories in John's account of the life of Jesus. One thing that makes him stand out is that he was incredibly taken with this young rabbi and wanted to introduce his friends to Jesus. His life would be a testimony of the effectiveness of witnessing to others about Jesus. Philip introduced Nathanael right away. He wasted no time getting others interested in the Christ.

Philip recognized immediately that the prophecy that Moses had recorded over 1,400 years earlier was being fulfilled in front of him. Philip knew Jesus was the Messiah. He even spoke plainly to his friend and according to John said, "We have found the one that Moses wrote in the Law and also the Prophets wrote, this Jesus of Nazareth, the son of Joseph." Philip was firmly convinced from the start of his relationship with Jesus that there was no doubt of His authenticity.

Philip's calling by Jesus was special. It was personal. It was direct. It was intentional. The evidence supported by the Gospel of John indicates that Jesus was not then limited to one method of finding His disciples, nor is He today. As a Christian, you receive God's calling, not because of your own effort. It is not because of your strength, talents, abilities, or skills.

God calls to you through the Holy Spirit, and then you have the ability to choose that faith in Him through His Son Jesus.

Some scholars believe that Philip was a disciple of John the Baptist, who was the second cousin physically to Jesus, because they lived in the same area where John preached. He was a Galilean, and more than likely knew well both Peter and Andrew.

When Philip told Nathanael about Jesus, there was obvious skepticism about Philip's claim. But Jesus satisfied that doubt when He told Nathanael that He had been watching him sitting under a fig tree before Philip even approached him. No one but Nathanael would have known where he was or what he was doing. Yet, Jesus did.

The town of Nazareth was considered by everyone to be proverbially wicked. If you were a Nazarene, you brought the same evil reputation of Nazareth with you. People thought of Nazareth with contempt and disdain. There was a distinct prejudice against anyone who came from that area. But that is from where Jesus came. As well, Bethsaida had a similar dislike by the population. Actually, Jesus denounced that city because of their unbelief. But Philip, and probably Nathanael, hailed from there.

God used something bad to do something good.

Philip is largely an unknown commodity to scholars. Matthew, Mark, and Luke's Gospels provide no details about him. All the Bible scenes about Philip appear in the Gospel of John. However, from that book, he appears to be a completely different kind of person than Peter, Andrew, James, or John. Often Philip is paired with Nathanael, whom he brought to Jesus.

The difficulty with building a biography of Philip, or for that matter most of the other disciples, is that their stories appear primarily in religious writings such as the New Testament and various apocryphal books. There are no known secular non-Biblical or historical sources to corroborate any of their accounts. Believers in western Christian civilization, however, have trusted these stories for almost two thousand years.

Regardless, one attribute that was certain is that Philip was an early adopter. He jumped into the deep end of the pool of knowledge and acceptance of Jesus. There was no lag time or hesitation. He believed. He trusted. He engaged. He followed. Did he completely comprehend all that would be required of him as a disciple? Probably not, at least not at the beginning of their journey together. As time passed, Philip would remain faithful, if at times a bit apprehensive of how things would work out.

It is possible Philip would have been at the wedding in Cana when Jesus performed His first miracle of turning water into wine. He would have seen the interaction between Mary and her son, and with the wedding party. Philip would have been amazed at the power that it took for creating one beverage from another.

He would have questioned how that could have been done, and perhaps would have been somewhat confused at how it happened. How could a man change the chemical composition of an everyday liquid like water into a more complex structure like wine. What powers did Jesus have that no one else did?

It was only the day before that, when along with the other disciples, Philip was questioning Jesus on where they would get enough food to feed 5,000 people. He was ever so practical in his calculations of how much money it would take to feed everyone, and that they didn't have that much cash on hand. After all, it would have taken two hundred days of wages to even come close to purchasing what they needed to accomplish this task. Impossible!

Additionally, it would appear from John's account of the Feeding of the 5,000 that Philip may have been in charge of the supplies and food. He was a rational kind of guy who was practical, perhaps acting like a crew chief for the team. Philip was concerned about the bottom line. He wanted to make sure all their bases were covered. Talk about supply chain issues! Philip no doubt was experiencing a crisis of confidence at that point when there was no food or no money, and a demanding crowd that needed to be satisfied.

Jesus was testing Philip's faith, and the disciple failed the test. All twelve learned a lesson that day, when instead of trusting in physical resources they were forced to recognize the spiritual nature of divine resources. Jesus had something else in mind when he questioned how they would feed the crowd. Philip saw firsthand that Jesus was definitely in tune with His Father.

Creating something gigantic out of nominal substance was well within His capabilities. Once blessed, there was no end to the amount of food Jesus created until every last person in the crowd had been satisfied. Plus, there were leftovers. Jesus' compassion on his audience was without equal. The enormity of the provisions was beyond their comprehension. Philip definitely learned trust and faith, and it would come in handy only a few hours later.

The Bible does not record any interaction or participation by Philip in the story about Peter and his nighttime jaunt on the Sea of Galilee. It is assumed that he would have been in the boat with Peter and the rest of the Twelve as they were just instructed by Jesus to cross over to the other side after this gargantuan meal. Philip, probably like the others, was exhausted from their attempts to cross the lake in the windstorm. As well, he was also frightened out of his mind like the others when they imagined a ghost bearing down on them in the deep watch of the night.

Philip was definitely part of the crowd during the Sea of Galilee adventure. He was involved doing his part rowing with all his might to accomplish the task that Jesus had given them. Unfortunately, their progress was being denied by nature.

Hearing the comforting words of the Messiah hopefully had help to calm his spirit, but Philip still needed another lesson in faith. His trust in Jesus was going to be significantly enhanced at the conclusion of their journey. Until then, he needed to learn that faith requires absolute trust.

Frightened just like the others in the boat that dreadful night on the water, Philip knew that once Jesus identified Himself to them He would not forsake them. Once the Messiah showed up, He showed Philip and the others that He was able to rescue not only a foolish and anxious Peter from drowning, but also the twelve together as a group.

His divine mastery over nature must have been quite a shocking sight to the practicality of Philip. He noticed that the out of control winds came under control when Jesus spoke. Was Philip's belief in the Messiah strengthened that night? At least, this disciple saw a mighty miracle which gave him courage.

Philip was curious to learn as much about Jesus and his teachings as he could. During the last night before the betrayal by Jesus when they were all together celebrating the Passover, and what has historically been called the Last Supper, Philip made a bold request. John's gospel says that he wanted to know more about God. *"Master, show us the Father, and that will be enough for us."*

Surprised by his statement, Jesus replied,, *"Have I been with you for so long a time and you still do not know me, Philip? Whoever has seen me has seen the Father."* The verbal exchange between Jesus and Philip shows that Believers are called to grow daily in faith. Philip evidently had not yet made the connection about Jesus and God. But none of others had connected the dots either. They would need to see Him after the crucifixion and the resurrection to fully understand what Jesus meant. They would be spiritually enlightened when their hearts' eyes were opened.

Philip would have further reason to believe in Jesus as they grew closer in time to the end of Jesus' earthly ministry. As the appointed hour of the crucifixion and death of Christ became a realistic possibility, Philip would need to reach deep into his personal reservoir of faith to overcome the anxiety and fear of what would happen, not only to Jesus, but also to him and the other disciples. These life lessons he was experiencing as part of his spiritual growth with Jesus would serve him well once the Great Commission was given to the disciples.

What eventually happened to Philip? After receiving the Holy Spirit at Pentecost, he reportedly traveled to Asia Minor, now commonly known as Turkey to preach about Jesus. According to church history, Philip was a martyr for his faith. He laid his life down for Christ, being stoned to death after reaching many with the gospel. However, in extra-biblical and apocryphal traditions, there are a couple different stories about how Philip died.

In some traditions, he simply died of old age. However, in more popular traditions, Philip died a martyr's death by crucifixion. According to the tradition recounted in the gnostic apocryphal book *"Acts of Philip",* Philip was persecuted by the Roman Empire because he was responsible for converting people to Christianity. Under the reign of Roman Emperor Domitian around 80 A.D., he was crucified in Hierapolis, Egypt. Like Peter, Philip was crucified upside down. He did not feel worthy and did not want to be crucified in the same way as Jesus.

Chapter Eleven – The Doubter

Thomas, known as the doubter, has been given a bad rap by most everyone since his infamous Missouri like "Show me" statement shortly after Jesus's resurrection. After all, wasn't he the one who said he wouldn't accept the fact that his beloved Messiah had come back from death itself? Didn't he cast heavy sarcasm and disdain on the eyewitness statements of those disciples who saw the empty tomb?

Talk about a guy who deserved the title. Imagine him in a little fishing boat at night in the middle of a raging tempest, rowing for all he's worth to get from one side to the other. Then you see a mystical, ethereal image headed right toward you. My guess is that his doubt was at an all time high right about the time that Jesus was approaching this motley crew. He probably couldn't believe his eyes. Thomas surely could not imagine a man coming to them on top of the water. Who is this person who can defy the laws of nature?

After all, the Sea of Galilee is a big lake, with a maximum depth of 141 feet and a surface area of over 64 square miles. It was a huge area of commerce during the New Testament era days. Anyone who wanted to cross over would do so by boat, not walking. That was physically impossible and unbelievable. The only possible explanation of this overnight event was that whomever was approaching Thomas and the others was a spirit of some kind. Doubt always leads to fear.

Thomas has been labeled the doubter because of his disbelief in the testimonies of those who went to Jesus' empty tomb after the resurrection. Unfortunately, even though his disbelief turned to belief upon seeing the Jesus after he entered into the place where the disciples had gathered to talk about the events of the day, this moniker was to haunt his legacy ever since those statements of doubt.

He was the only disciple of the remaining group, minus Judas Iscariot, who was not with them when Jesus first appeared after he rose from the dead. Imagine his emotions after seeing the torture that the Messiah endured, from the Roman flogging to the crucifixion and his burial in a sealed and guarded tomb all within 24 hours. That would cause a toll on anyone who had just lost their spiritual leader. His faith had been shattered.

Thomas had experienced moments of bravery during Jesus' ministry when he said they should accompany Him back to see Lazarus to the place where the Jewish leaders had planned to stone Jesus to death. Thomas almost takes on a trait similar to Peter. Ironically, he appeared to have more faith in Jesus than the other disciples. Thomas is often quoted with a cynical tone. Yet, he may have been one of the more courageous disciples.

That was one of his better moments, but his doubt about Jesus being alive again was one of his lowest points in life. Like all who live, each person experiences times when they shine, and times when their light seems to be the dimmest. When Thomas was at his weakest point, Jesus showed up to dispel the mystery behind His resurrection, and Thomas' disbelief became belief.

There's no doubt Thomas' doubts would have been alleviated quicker if he had simply been with the rest of the disciples as they gathered together the first time when Jesus showed up. The lesson from the scripture about Thomas here is that being in the presence of Jesus brought out the best in him by increasing his faith.

The opposite was that being away from Jesus seemed to trigger doubt and lack of faith. Indeed, he was having a hard time recovering from the shock they had all just experienced within the previous week.

There is more to Thomas, though, than most people know. There's a good chance that Thomas was a twin. John's gospel records that Thomas was known as "Didymus," the Greek word for twin. Interestingly enough as well, the name Thomas also means twin in Aramaic, which was the common language throughout Palestine in the first century. In that case, to stand out from his sibling, he may have had to constantly make himself known and to question what he believed. He was a skeptic, but maybe for good reason. It strengthened his belief.

Asking questions is a good thing in most cases. It helps you get clarity and provides answers. Asking questions helps to obtain insights and understanding. If Thomas was doubting the others about Jesus either during the storm on the Sea of Galilee, or in the room after the resurrection, he was seeking the truth. Only Jesus provided that to him. Thomas knew the other disciples well enough to be wary of some of their statements and their actions.

After all, they were all human, and humans make mistakes. But Jesus was patient with each of them.

Thomas did not see Jesus for a full week after he had doubted the claims by the other disciples that Jesus was alive. He was thinking about their words, yet he was still unsure. He needed proof. After all, why hadn't Jesus shown Himself to him, and when did Jesus plan to come back to them even if He was alive again. Seeking answers was what drove Thomas to question his faith as well as life itself. He, like the others, was likely very afraid of what might happen to them.

John's gospel continues to unfold the story about Thomas. *"A week later his disciples were in the house again, and Thomas was with them. Though the doors were locked, Jesus came and stood among them and said, 'Peace be with you!" Then he said to Thomas, "Put your finger here; see my hands. Reach out your hand and put it into my side. Stop doubting and believe'"* (John 20:26–27, NIV).

Jesus was not chastising Thomas for his lack of faith. Rather, He addressed Thomas in a way that allowed him to believe in a gentle and reassuring manner. The importance of this lesson is that even though Thomas had been with Jesus for three years and had seen Him perform many miracles, including walking on water, he still struggled to believe. Believers who have their faith challenged on a regular basis know that doubts creep in to shake the trust they have in Christ.

Jesus treats everyone who knows Him with the same gentleness of spirit.

Nowhere does the Bible say whether or not Thomas physically touched Jesus' wounds. Catholic tradition holds that Thomas did actually touch the holes in his flesh. This belief historically supported the idea of using physical rituals and pilgrimages to bolster faith. Conversely, Protestant tradition supports that Thomas did *not* touch them, reinforcing the idea that faith alone is enough for salvation. This theological difference is often represented in Catholic and Protestant art portraying Jesus and Thomas.

The Bible does record that Thomas was among the few disciples fishing with Peter after the resurrection. They were again struggling through the night. This time the wind was not the culprit, but the fish. Their lack of faith was evident, and their efforts were in vain. Was it because they had not consulted God in their prayers to seek His will, or was it because that was where they felt comfortable. They had returned to a life before Jesus, and now they were afraid of failure again.

When Jesus showed up at their original encounter with Thomas and the others, He made them uncomfortable throughout their three year journey together. All of the disciples doubted at some point, and all of them lacked faith along the way. Thomas was just more vocal than the others when it came to not believing…. Until he believed. During the breakfast on the shore of the Sea of Galilee, He made them uncomfortable again by asking what they were doing and then revealing Himself to them as the risen Christ.

Even though Jesus repeatedly revealed his plans to the disciples, they never understood the cross and resurrection until after the fact. Plus, as Jewish men, they had no reason to believe the Messiah would be resurrected. It was out of the scope of contemporary thought and reason.

The resurrection of Jesus went against everything Thomas and the rest of them understood and believed about the Messiah—and death—since they were children. It smacked completely against their tradition. Despite everything the twelve heard and saw that proved Jesus was not like anyone who ever lived, He died just like everyone else.

Thomas has been given a bad rap for doubting. His disbelief did not originate out of pride, but instead more from a state of deep grief, painful to the inner core of his being. He had just lost a close friend and the One whom he believed to be the Messiah. He was shaken, profoundly sad, and incredibly disappointed in the outcome of their faith journey.

Judging Thomas and his story is somewhat unfair looking back two millennia. Jesus knew Thomas, and He understood the grief and pain he was feeling. His disciple's heart was burdened and heavy with care.

It is no wonder that Thomas doubted the resurrection until he saw the evidence for himself. And Jesus' willingness to engage Thomas in the midst of his doubts encourages Believers today to also bring their doubts to Him. It's important to recognize that in Jesus' response to Thomas, He recognized how much harder it would be for anyone who had never seen His miracles to believe. Showing His scars to Thomas was a sign of compassion. Jesus wanted him to believe, to strengthen his faith, and to encourage his belief in Jesus as God and Savior.

After the ascension of Jesus to Heaven, church tradition reported that Thomas began teaching the gospel of Christ in the lands east of Israel. The stories in large part are told in the apocryphal testament *"The Acts of Thomas"* written in the early third century, which was largely deemed not credible and unworthy to be included of part of the New Testament.

The earliest mention of Thomas' missionary work comes from Eusebius of Caesarea, who quotes third century scholar Origen, as saying that Thomas was sent to Parthia (which is in modern day Iran). However, according to more popular church tradition, Thomas journeyed to India around 50 AD. The common supposition is that he evangelized the people there, possibly establishing as many as at least seven churches.

Christians in India are very convinced that Thomas came to the southern part of that country, especially with the large number of churches located there. Churches were named after him, and Christians in India claim that he was there, although is impossible to prove or disprove. It is reported Thomas was killed there by a spear from a disbeliever. He gave his life for the sake of the Gospel as did his friends and fellow disciples.

Chapter Twelve – Little Jimmy

James the Less, possibly Matthew's brother, had a father by the same name Alphaeus who also was called Clopas. And his mother was also named Mary. James was hand-picked by Jesus to be a disciple, and he was present with the disciples in the last Passover supper in Jerusalem. He may have been the first disciple to see the Jesus after His resurrection. He was a Galilean from Capernaum.

James did not seek recognition or fame, and he received no glory or credit for his service to Christ. He, like each of these twelve men, sacrificed everything they knew and held dear to follow Him. James and the others gave up their jobs, their homes, their friends, their families and everything that was comfortable and familiar to them to answer the calling that Jesus placed on their lives.

James was an ordinary man who was allowed to do extraordinary things for the cause of Christ. He served as an example of someone willing to fully commit to the service of God. James was an unsung hero for his faith.

Although his accomplishments remain largely unknown, James may simply have been overshadowed by the disciples who played a more prominent presence in the New Testament. However, being named among the twelve was no small achievement. James the Less was considered as a close friend and co-worker in the faith during his time in ministry with the Messiah for those three and a half years. Even though he did not get a lot of attention in the gospels, he nonetheless was part of the group closest to Jesus.

In Mark's gospel, he uses a word to describe James that means small in stature. It could indicate that he was little. It also can mean young in age. It could mean that he was both. It also could mean that he was least in influence. He didn't have a powerful personality, and he wasn't a tall, strapping heroic looking guy. And he certainly was not the oldest in the crowd. So, James possibly was little, and young, and not very influential – "Little Jimmy."

The Bible really does not say much about James the Less. There is no description of what he did, other than be present with Jesus and the disciples during their time together. There is no word on his testimony or his actions. He is not mentioned as being talkative or argumentative or even very active. Essentially, his role is based on obscurity.

Not everyone needs to be the center of attention. The scripture is largely silent on James, but he did have the opportunity to be part of the greatest group of men who ever lived. At the end of the day, perhaps it was his obedience and his faith that kept him involved.

Any study of James the son of Alphaeus is difficult because, other than his name, there is no single verse in the Bible that describes his life or service to the Messiah. The name "James" is actually a Greek rendering of the Hebrew name "Jacob". It was a popular name during the time of Christ and is still popular today. There are some scholars who believe he may have been Matthew's brother, but there is not enough solid evidence to support that opinion.

He was involved, though. He did participate. He was instrumental as part of the group to obey Jesus even though he didn't understand the instructions most of the time. He did what he was told. James was there in the middle of the crowds all the time, and he went with Jesus everywhere they traveled. James was a follower, and he excelled at that task. He was a servant to the Messiah and to the masses. His responsibility was to listen and obey, and that is undoubtedly what James did -- all the time.

It is unilaterally accepted that he was part of the feeding of the 5,000 and that he jumped into the boat to cross the Sea of Galilee afterward to go meet Jesus on the other side as he was instructed to do along with the other eleven disciples. And, like the others, he was struggling to row against the raging wind and water that night.

Nowhere is it recorded that he said anything on his own that night, but the Bible is pretty clear that all twelve of them screamed in horror and fright when they saw Jesus approaching the boat at three in the morning. James was part of the loud collective shriek. His fear was as common as the next man.

His awe of Jesus came from a natural respect of the man and His miracles. James was one of those men who observed the situation around him and learned from it. He didn't argue the point or challenge the status quo. He was one of the quietest of the group, but his opinion of Jesus was never in question. He may have been confused or uncertain at times based upon his understanding of Jewish customs and laws, but He never confronted Jesus or called Him out to prove Himself. James was committed.

James accepted Jesus. He would not have followed Him if there was any reason not to do so. He came into the realization that there was something significantly unique about the Messiah, and he was not about to abandon the cause. His faith was quiet. It was solid. It was definite. It was determined. Eventually, after the resurrection, his faith was eternally established. Little Jimmy may have been small in stature, but his faith was gigantic.

James the Less was definitely a background disciple. Yet he still saw and experienced the miracles, healings, teachings and fellowship with Jesus. He may have been unknown to many then and even today, but obscurity is not an indicator of the condition of your relationship between yourself and God. Some people are able to live life making great impressions on others by what they have accomplished.

The truth is that most individuals are quite average in comparison. Men and women live and die, and for the most part the world does not take notice and just moves on, typically forgetting those it leaves behind.

Quiet service to God is where James the Less made his mark. His faithfulness and his faith are what set him apart from the many others who wanted only their physical needs met from Jesus. He was humble and diligent as he patiently served Jesus. That is where many Believers fulfill their spiritual destiny. That kind of life goes unnoticed and unrecorded by mankind, but God sees the heart.

God rewards those who serve Him regardless of their circumstances.

There is a story about his life after Jesus and his demise as a disciple. It is said by various sources James preached in Syria. He would have been welcomed by those who fled persecution by the Romans and other Jewish religious authorities. He also would have had a wider audience based on the mixture of cultures that territory would have made up the population in the area. It was a major trading route. But supposedly he was stoned to death there by Jews who held his message about Jesus to be heretical to their faith.

The most reputable church tradition says that James went to Persia to preach the gospel. That area is today known as Iran. However, he was not received well there and was supposedly crucified. Here was an unknown preacher (a silent soldier) who was doing his Master's bidding and was killed for his faith in an area of the world even then that was wicked, brutal and vicious. It apparently has not changed in two millennia.

James' lasting legacy is his contribution to the expansion of the gospel eastward that left an indelible impression on the lives of people who were searching for hope in a dying world. The trade route that connected Jerusalem and Damascus to Iraq also allowed for the gospel to move east into India. Truly, this disciple was taking the good news of salvation to the uttermost parts of the known world.

James, son of Alphaeus, may go down in history as the obscure disciple. Truth be told, most of mankind lives in obscurity. However, he will still sit upon one of the twelves thrones of the apostles because Jesus never forgets. Along with the other disciples, James set in place a movement that formed the early foundations of Christianity and the church.

They began a movement that steadily spread around the globe. Believers today are still a part of that movement two thousand years later.

Chapter Thirteen – The First Martyr

James, brother to John, and was the first apostolic martyr for the cause of Christ, executed by Herod III. His father Zebedee raised a fiery, forceful young man, and his mother Salome wanted to make sure he had a premier position in Jesus' kingdom. He was one of the *"sons of thunder"* that also included his brother John. Evidently, James like his sibling was fiery and tempestuous. Jesus nicknamed them both "Boanerges", which is translated from Aramaic to mean how they were to be known.

James was likely loud and fervid in his character. Jesus knew him well, and gave him and his brother the moniker that fit them well. The literal meaning of this appellation is "sons of the tumult." Perhaps he was argumentative, and even somewhat headstrong. Certainly he was boisterous enough to stand out from the crowd. He was a fisherman, like his father and his brother.

They were at the Sea of Galilee preparing their nets to go out to fish when Jesus found this group. Interestingly, Jesus had just found Simon Peter and his brother Andrew fishing a short way up the road. Matthew's gospel records that both sets of brothers immediately left their nets – essentially their jobs, their livelihoods, their family, and their familiar surroundings – and followed Him.

I wonder what old Zeb thought when he saw his sons walk away with a total stranger. What feelings did he have about losing two thirds of his built in family work force? How was he going to survive with just a few hired men to help him? Where were they going, how long would they be gone, and would they ever return? James no doubt had complete faith in this man Jesus to leave everything he held dear to wander off thitout explanation or direction.

Would he communicate with his father during the three and a half years as a disciple? What was the reason he wanted to follow Jesus? James would later provide some answers, but for now he was headed out into the unknown with someone he didn't know to accomplish who knows what. His brother likely had the same thoughts. James was going to learn some powerful lessons while traveling with this rabbi.

Right away he began to notice something different about this itinerant Jewish teacher. They were quickly headlong into ministry with Jesus as they traveled together through the Galilean countryside. James began to witness Jesus accomplish miraculous events, including healing all manner of illnesses and issues both physical, mental and spiritual. Jesus was rapidly establishing a reputation far and wide as a healer, teacher, and preacher.

Crowds were flocking to Him to see Him, to hear Him, and to be healed by Him. James was there as an eyewitness to it all. What about his vociferous nature? Was he being bold enough to question the actions and activities of their group and its leader, or was he content to just observe the scenes as they unfolded around him?

The Bible is clear about some of James' comments concerning getting retribution on others. As you may think, James could be rash and very unsympathetically direct. He had an unthinking personality. He was not known to always apply the gospel to earthly matters. He did thunder forth on more than one occasion.

In one outlandish incident, James and John possessed some truly thunder-like qualities. Jesus and His disciples were traveling through Samaria on their way to Jerusalem when they ran into trouble. Jesus attempted to find accommodations for the night in one place but was met with opposition from the villagers, simply because His destination was Jerusalem. This attitude was the result of a long-standing reciprocal Jew and Samaritan prejudice. Fiercely loyal, James and his brother wanted to burn up a city when the people refused to welcome Jesus.

"When the disciples James and John saw this, they asked, 'Lord, do you want us to call fire down from heaven to destroy them?'". Jesus rebuked these thundering brothers as a way to teach them a lesson about humility and forgiveness. James and John's response to the Samaritans reveals a distinct fervency.

They were exhibiting an angry and impetuous nature that could properly be considered "thunderous". Although not disclosed in the scriptures, there were probably other times when James and John lived up to their nickname.

During his time serving as a woe begotten rower during the overnight trip across the Sea of Galilee, James was probably thinking that this journey should have been done during daylight hours. After all, he was familiar with the lake and knew it could be tricky navigating those waters in darkness.

Yet, he did what he was told when Jesus gave the order to head over to Capernaum on the other side. He had not calculated, however, on how long it would take, and his temper was more than likely roiling up more and more the longer and harder they tried. Even in the windstorm, James was probably exhibiting his own thunder.

James was also a spiritual bonehead before the crucifixion. He was still thinking Jesus would have an earthly royal kingdom ruling with His disciples. And James wanted to be at the top of the food chain when it came to management of Jerusalem and the Hebrew nation. Jesus had been pouring His heart out talking with the twelve about His impending death. He had been telling these men what was going to happen to Him and what they should expect.

Then James comes out with a ridiculous question almost like he wasn't paying attention to the subject. It was as if he was completely clueless to the emotion of the moment and the incredible activities that were coming to pass. James selfishly asks Jesus, *"'Teacher,' they said, 'we want you to do for us whatever we ask. ... Let one of us sit at your right and the other at your left in your glory.'"* I can just imagine the look on Jesus' face when he hears this statement. You know He has to think "Wait….What!?"

Jesus doesn't completely lose His cool at this moment, but He certainly calls them to task for being so spiritually stupid. He rebuked both of them, asking if they were ready to drink from the cup He was going to drink from and saying the honor was not even for Him to grant. The other disciples were definitely annoyed with

James and his brother. How insanely dull witted and insensitive! Who put him up to this question, and why did he think it was appropriate to ask at such a sensitive moment in Jesus' life.

The Messiah was constantly teaching James and the others that the greatest calling of a being His servant was to serve others. James discovered that following Jesus can lead to hardship, persecution, and even death, but the reward is spending eternity with Him in Heaven. The disciples were continuing to desire greatness, but Jesus was all about serving, ministry and deliverance from sin. His role was to help James understand who Jesus was in order for James to understand who he was. Jesus had called James to follow and to serve.

When someone is called to faith in Christ, their next step should be to find out what God wants them to do, where to serve, and how to be more like Jesus.

Believers have the responsibility to learn as much as they can about who Jesus is, and how their lives belong to Him. The Bible says that Christians no longer belong to themselves. They are bought with a price. James, like the others, thought he knew himself. Jesus turned his life around and showed him how much he did not know in order for James to learn who he needed to be.

James was also called "James, the Great" to distinguish him from another disciple with the same name, the brother of Jesus, who is usually called James the Just or James the Lesser. Jesus' brother James is traditionally believed to be the author of the Book of James in the New Testament, and he became known as a pillar of the early Christian church along with Peter and John, son of Zebedee.

James, the brother of Jesus, was a major leader in the church in Jerusalem. The title "the greater" doesn't necessarily mean James, son of Zebedee, was more important than James the Just. The suggestion and understanding is that his title just indicates that he was possibly the oldest or tallest of the two. It was a common understanding in Biblical days.

James, however, in spite of his overzealous behavior and vocabulary did have some shining moments in his life with Jesus. These outspoken "sons of thunder" were also invited into Jesus' inner circle of disciples. James and John, along with Peter, accompanied Jesus when He raised Jairus' daughter from the dead. James saw the little girl come to life while everyone else was shut outside, as recorded in Matthew's Gospel account. James and his brother were on the mountain when Jesus was transfigured.

James firsthand was able to spend time with Moses and Elijah in the presence of a glorified Jesus. He saw Jesus in His full divine glory transfigured in front of him. He heard the voice of God – something that most humans had never experienced. That, indeed, was a mountaintop experience in every sense of the word. Imagine being in the presence of the most respected and revered men in all of Jewish literature and history, as well as seeing the Son of God in His glorious state.

As if it wasn't enough that all of his senses had been heightened to a new dimension, James experiences audible proof of the existence of the Ancient of Days, the God of Abraham, Isaac and Jacob, the voice of the great "I AM." Simply amazing.

No doubt the hair on the back of his neck was standing straight up. At once fearful and awestruck, James was one of only three men to ever visibly encounter men who were no longer living appear alive in front of him, and to enjoy the conversation they were having with the One who was alive before Abraham.

During the Passion Week after Jesus and the disciples were in Jerusalem, James was one of the few disciples who were able to learn a significant teaching about the end of the age. James heard eschatological comments from Jesus that would confuse even the most brilliant of scholars, yet he was given the opportunity to hear what the God of the universe had planned for all mankind and creation.

Additionally, even though James fell asleep when he was supposed to be praying and watching during the night, Jesus took him with Him when He wrestled in prayer the night of His arrest in the Garden of Gethsemane after their last Passover meal together.

James, like the others, had some definite highs and lows in his walk with Jesus. His life with the Master prepared him for what was to come soon after Jesus went to Heaven. He finally realized that the Messiah had a spiritual kingdom in mind, and James would be part of it.

A decade after the martyrdom of Stephen, King Herod Agrippa was appointed governor of Judea by the Roman political hierarchy. In an effort to establish himself in the good graces of his people, Herod Agrippa ordered a blazing persecution against all Christians. He was determined to make a substantial impact by striking down the most prominent Christian leaders, including James.

The site of martyrdom – the only one recorded in the New Testament - is located within the Armenian Cathedral of Saint James in the Armenian Quarter of Jerusalem according to their tradition. The Chapel of Saint James the Great, located to the left of the sanctuary, is the traditional place where he was martyred, when King Herod Agrippa I of Judea ordered him to be beheaded as written about in the New Testament Book of Acts.

Additionally, a notable primitive writer of early church history, Clemens Alexandrinus, gave an extra-Biblical account of his death that includes drama, repentance by his accuser, forgiveness, and a dual execution of both James and his newly born again Christian brother.

His head is said to be buried under the altar, marked by a piece of red marble and surrounded by six votive lamps. According to Spanish tradition, his body was taken to Santiago de Compostela, where his shrine attracts Christian pilgrims from all over the world. James is traditionally regarded as the Patron saint of Spain

Chapter Fourteen – Son of Thunder

John, brother to James, and the younger son to Zebedee and his wife Salome, was the other "son of thunder." John and his brother James were among the first disciples called by Jesus. According to Mark's gospel account, John is typically mentioned after James and was probably the younger brother.

He was the other Boanerges brother, called out by the Messiah perhaps because of some character trait such as the zeal he exemplified; and his mother was among those women who ministered to the circle of disciples who closely followed Jesus.

Many readers of the New Testament see John as a gentle loving soul who would do no harm and only preach about love. However, there was another side to him, especially in his early years with Jesus, that shows his elitist and selfish side.

He had an explosive nature like his brother, and together they showed themselves to be overly zealous when it came to each wanting his own way. He was no quiet, unassuming man. In his younger years, John was headstrong and a schemer.

He also had little sympathy for others, including those he felt were beneath his station in life. Was that due to his father's successful fishing business and a sense of entitlement, or possibly it was based on his status as a Hebrew and recognition as a member of God's chosen people for the last few thousand years?

Whatever reason caused him to react toward others in an often explosive and callous manner would later be tempered as he grew in spiritual maturity and age. His egotistical attitude eventually gave way to a tremendous turnaround in his behavior and his spirit.

The longer he was with the "Lamb of God," the more John became like Jesus, which should be the desire of every Believer.

During the harrowing night on the Sea of Galilee when Jesus had told him and the others to launch out and meet Him on the other side, John was as curious as the rest of disciples before they all left the shore, and as fearful as the rest of them when Jesus approached them in the fourth watch of the night on the water. Did he scream in fright along with the group, or was his reaction different from them? Since most men were ripe with superstition in those days, it is probable that John was as guilty as the other men.

Only Peter was ambitious enough to jump ship. John did not, nor did any of the other disciples. John stayed in the boat. He was tired. He was afraid. He was worn out. He was unsure of this apparent apparition. His need to be fearless had evaporated like the night mist created by the rampant waves against their craft. Jesus, however, knew that John needed Him.

Jesus knew that John would one day be one of the greatest survivors of the early church and be responsible for some of the world's greatest literature. He knew John would be a guardian of truth, a proponent of faith, and an example to Believers for over two thousand years.

Although John was lacking faith during their overnight boat ride, Jesus was aware that John's faith in Him would grow. John would turn out to be precious to Jesus, and like the rest of the disciples, need His continued personal training in faith and obedience. There was a reason that John became known as the most beloved of all the disciples. John was living a life that had much to gain in character development. His mood swing would be one of the biggest accomplishments of his life, going from a hater to a lover of all mankind.

Jesus saw the potential in John, even when this disciple was unaware of his need for Jesus.

Along with James and Peter, John was one of Jesus' closest confidants, so he appears in more biblical accounts than the other disciples. He probably saw Jesus turn the water into wine at a wedding in Cana as the first recorded miracle. He was with Jesus when He raised a little girl from the dead who was the daughter of a man named Jairus.

John was present at the mountaintop experience during Jesus' transfiguration, along with his brother James and with Peter. He was closest to Jesus during the Passover supper and the journey afterward to the Garden of Gethsemane.

John was present at the crucifixion of Jesus, and three days later he was the first to arrive at the empty tomb. He did, indeed, believe that his Master had risen from the dead. John was the first one to recognize Jesus on the shore of the Sea of Galilee after the resurrection, and he became very well known in the early church after Pentecost.

Even Paul recognized John as one of the primary disciples. John outlived his contemporaries, and as a result was able to establish a significant role as a pillar of early Christian writing and thought. His brother James was the first of the disciples to die, and John was the last. They were the living bookends to the first "fishers of men."

John was not a stranger to his share of grief. James, his brother, who also walked with Jesus and who also shared the overnight boat ride on the lake, saw Jesus perform miracles. James was martyred for sharing his testimony to others. But John continued to live on and proclaim the gospel, the same one for which his brother lost his life. John likely grieved over that personal loss for the rest of his life.

The ministry John participated in with Jesus was definitely a family related experience. His father's business was affected by John's discipleship, and his brother James gave up his life for it. John was given watch care over Mary, the mother of Jesus, by Him as He was dying on the cross. The two families were permanently bonded by these mutual occurrences.

Watching his leader, his rabbi, his friend, and his Messiah be tortured by death caused by crucifixion must have been the most horrible scene he ever witnessed. And, he lived many long years to tell about it. John's words in his New Testament writings have had significant impact on unknown billions of individuals since he penned them.

John's home and family were transformed by his relationship with Jesus. His faith became a live out loud kind of belief. Jesus and John were meant to be together for those three and a half years in order for the gospel to be told for the future benefit of every person who has ever lived since then.

John never called himself by his name in any of his writings. He referred to himself always as "the disciple whom Jesus loved." Starting out as a man who had a problem with his attitudes towards others, he became truly a unique individual that was concerned only about loving Jesus and loving others.

The closeness of his relationship as a disciple with the Messiah turned into one of ultimate trust at the crucifixion. At that critical moment in history, John was the only disciple to hear the last words Jesus would ever utter before His death on the cross.

John is traditionally regarded as authoring five books in the New Testament including the Gospel of John, the epistles listed as 1 John, 2 John, and 3 John, and the Book of Revelation. However, some Bible scholars dispute which of these he actually wrote. John is also believed to be the only disciple who died of old age. The remaining others were allegedly martyred according to church tradition.

Although there are prophecies about the end of days that are written in the Old Testament, only John was in the history of mankind the only person to see the future and get a glimpse of Heaven. The role that he would play in the development of prophetic scripture is instrumental in the understanding Believers have of eschatology, which is the study of the end of the world and the ultimate destiny of humanity.

John was the catalyst of discipleship and ushered into the new sect known as Christians the believability of how God plans the Second

Coming of Jesus, the last Judgement, the resurrection of the dead, the end of Satan, and the final kingdom of the Son of David on earth.

John's writing, especially in the Book of Revelation, denotes a finality of evil in the cosmos. His epistles also spell out how Believers are to deal with each other in the interim. His Gospel account of Jesus shines gloriously as a testimony of salvation, grace and mercy. It also provides the world the reason for God's love of His creation including mankind.

Some ancient sources may refer to the John called the Apostle by several other names including John of Patmos (largely due to his banishment to the island of Patmos by the Roman government), John the Elder, John the Divine, and the Beloved Disciple. He was one of Jesus' closest followers, and he witnessed more of Jesus' ministry than almost anyone else. The early Christian church leaned on his insight into the life and teachings of Christ for these reasons. Even leaders like Paul appealed to John's authority.

John found life and joy in Jesus. His writings are full of both. He wrote about truth. He wrote about faith. He wrote about grace and mercy. He also wrote about the future and how God's plan for mankind has an eternal impact and resolution for His glory.

He told those stories in his gospel for the purpose of leading others to a saving faith like he had. It was not about religion with John, or even a crusade or cause. It wasn't even about having his dreams fulfilled. John, and the other disciples who stayed faithful, found life in a person.

Their fellowship was with Jesus, not a denomination. So should yours be as a relationship and not a religion.

Chapter Fifteen – So Zealous

Simon the Zealot, who was a warrior at heart, had a strong desire to overthrow the Roman oppressors who were occupying his homeland at the time of Jesus. Zealots were all out against any force occupying their homeland. The nation of Israel had been established by God Himself by His covenant agreement with Abraham many generations before the reign of any Caesar. Who would dare try to rule a people that had a divine right and mandate to exist without the approval of man.

Simon is called in some Bible translations the Cananaean, which comes from the Aramaic word for the word "zealot." In old English, it is translated "Canaanite." In more modern translations, the word that is used to describe him is indeed "Zealot."

Bible scholars disagree whether he was truly a member of the radical political element, or that his religious zeal was so strong that Simon would be a natural fit for this band of brothers who would follow Jesus. Essentially, the original word means to be zealous for the law. Simon was both at the same time, for his faith and against his oppressors.

If you hold to the belief that Simon was politically charged, then he would have made a great balance counter to the role that Matthew the tax collector had. Simon was a hater of the Romans, and Matthew was sold out to them for his job. The former hated Romans and taxes, and the latter was employed by them and collected taxes for a living. Assuming that was the case for these two diametrically opposed men in theory, in reality it displays the irony that Jesus provided in His calling. His kingdom reaches out to everyone regardless of their social or political standing.

Jesus' love and mercy cover all who believe no matter their differences.

Simon, as a Zealot, had taken an oath to defeat any of those people at any cost and by any means necessary. His desire to rid Israel of the Roman government and its military forces was paramount above all other matters in life. He would do everything he could to further the cause of the Zealots to remove this pagan rule.

He likely felt that Jesus was destined to fulfill that role. He was incredibly popular with the citizenry and always had huge crowds following Him everywhere He went. At times they were overwhelming. Simon saw this as a definite advantage in his desire to remove Rome from the Jewish equation.

In Simon's mind, this unassuming Rabbi who spoke with truth and power, who performed miracles and appeared to know their history more than any other person, who was able to defy even the Jewish religious aristocracy without remorse was destined to be the Messiah who would drive out the imperial forces and rule with an iron fist as Israel's new king.

This disciple would soon learn that the kingdom he was imagining and the Kingdom that Jesus spoke about to them were two vastly different environments – physical versus spiritual, human versus divine, temporary versus eternal.

Not only did Simon have a possible political opposition to Jerusalem's overlords, but as a Zealot he would have also been religiously aligned with the Pharisees. Each of these groups saw eye to eye regarding the strict observance of Mosaic law. Since Jesus often called them out and had several run ins with this religious crowd, it is unique that He would have included Simon as part of the closest clan around Him.

But Jesus saw through religious and political agendas into the hearts of men. He recognized Simon for his true colors of belief and faith. Now, He just needed to mold him into His likeness for the time they were together.

Perhaps the reason that Simon wanted to be close to Jesus was to learn how to overthrow the Roman government. He reasonably would think that the Messiah would have a game plan that would provide a way to defeat the conquerors who were so destined to be in charge.

The Romans ability to occupy Israel was so total in its effect that no known uprising had yet been successful. However, with the right person who would be recognized as their new national hero, and who would be seen as the long-awaited Messiah prophesied from ancient times, may have the ability to rally the people and lead them to victory.

Simon would want to know Jesus's thoughts, His secrets, His wisdom, His talents and gifts, and His capacity to speak as One with authority. As a Zealot, this disciple would learn what Jesus knew and put it to good use. He would listen and observe. He would work hard to form a cohesive bond with the other eleven in this tight knit group of followers.

Simon would consider all their hardships as a path to victory. They would endure. They would succeed. They would be victorious. They would lead. They would be respected. They would be heroes in the sight of Israel and rule the land instead of those pesky, troublesome, horrible, tortuous invaders – those Romans.

Simon was probably waiting for the right time to overthrow the current government in Jerusalem. He could have been plotting all along to gain the trust of the others to help him in forming a plot to move against the regime held in place by the current governor, Pontius Pilate.

Knowing that the region was a powder keg ready to blow up at any moment, Simon also would be hoping for his leader to give the word. He must have been incredibly patient. So far, Jesus was only talking about peace and love, not about violent action against oppressive rulers. Would it come soon? He could only hope.

However, it would not be this night. His focus during the trip across the lake was only on getting to the other side without drowning. He would be rowing feverishly for hours on end, and even though the trip wasn't that far, the destination seemed like it was still far away.

Were they still not far from their launching point because the equipment and effort were faulty, or were they just unable to get across because of the violence of the storm. Either way, it appeared that the struggle was real.

Jesus chose each of the disciples for a specific reason, based on their background, their character, and for their willingness to follow someone who commanded respect. Simon the Zealot was one of those, and he had a personality type that evidently caused Jesus to take notice.

His statement, "You have not chosen me, but I have chosen you..," spoken to the disciples in John's gospel account spells out why Simon and the others were specifically selected out of all the thousands of men who lived around the Sea of Galilee in those days.

Jesus also appointed each of them to take His message to a lost and dying world. He commanded them to go, and He told them what to do – bear fruit. That meant, each of the disciples had a role to fulfill once they were called. Jesus has an appointment with all Believers, and He commands you to carry it out. This commandment, or appointment, refers in part to the fruit of the Spirit.

When you choose to bear fruit, your character as a Christian is steadily and incrementally transformed into the image of God's Son.

However, Jesus was more specifically speaking about bearing fruit of active ministry. His disciples are called to permit Jesus to work through them to continue His work of saving the lost and training more disciples. This kind of fruit is eternal. It is significant. It does not die away or get lost in translation. The fruit that these disciples were encouraged to develop was a major part of their future ministry.

So it is today to those who follow Christ. Your fruit as a Christian is to reproduce yourself in others so they may also become more like Him. Beyond salvation and spending eternity in Heaven beginning someday, the goal of Christian life is to bear fruit. Jesus was the ultimate judge of character. He saw an intensity in Simon the Zealot that would work well in spreading the gospel. Simon would be an excellent fruit bearer when his time came to produce.

There is not much evidence as to his final years, although it is known from the Book of Acts that he was present to vote on a replacement for Judas Iscariot. His involvement in spreading the gospel message after Jesus's ascension is largely based on some varying church traditions. All of the disciples remained faithful until their untimely deaths as martyrs. Only John outlived all of them into his elder years.

The majority of Bible scholars and religious historians believe Simon worked together with Judas Thaddeus to preach and spread the gospel into Egypt and parts of Persia. Fourth Century Bishop and writer Eusebius and second century Christian writer Hegesippus both independently wrote that Simon became the second bishop of the church in Jerusalem and that he was eventually martyred after that by the Roman Emperor Trajan in the late first or early second century. These are largely stories based on hearsay but are the closest, most reliable sources from that era. Regardless of his end, Simon was zealous for Jesus.

You may ask why Simon and his counterparts were so compelled to follow Jesus, and then to continue to spread His message of repentance, salvation and hope of eternal life knowing that the consequences for them could be difficult at best and their own death sentence at worst. They all learned together at Jesus' feet. They lived with Him, walked with Him, ate with Him, wept with Him, and found redemption eventually in Him.

Together, they huddled in a crowded fishing boat as Jesus calmed stormy seas. They watched Him walk on water. Together, they watched Him cure people of unclean disease and give sight to the blind. They saw Him raise the dead and cast out demons.

Together, these disciples heard Jesus teach with power that was authoritative and powerfully life changing. They saw him arrested without justice, secretly tried at night, beaten to a pulp and nailed to a cross. And together they witnessed Jesus alive again after He rose from the grave complete with nail-scarred hands, feet and all… Just as He promised.

Chapter Sixteen – The Traitor

Judas, came from a portion of Judea known as Kerioth, and his father Simon had the Iscariot moniker as an identifying trait, common in those days for indicating from where you came. He was a Judean, not a Galilean as were the rest of the disciples. Later, Judas would have this incorporated as part of his name as well. Judas Iscariot's life was tragic from the beginning of his association with Jesus until the bitter end. He would live a tortured life that was always involved for the wrong reasons.

Judas was almost exclusively interested in financial gain. He was the treasurer of the group and kept the purse close at hand, guarding it with his life. In those days, most of the population was dirt poor. The disciples were no less different. Each of them, with the possible exception of Matthew, did not have much to their name in the way of possessions.

That's why Judas really had more interest in money than in anything Jesus had to say. He knew that as the finance guy, he could dip into the till and not be suspected of stealing. Somehow he was able to convince the disciples that he was credible and trustworthy.

Except for the Apostle John. Though Judas isn't mentioned nearly as much during Jesus' ministry, the Bible does record that he was the treasurer for the disciples as recorded in John's Gospel. However, the Bible also reveals that Judas used this position for his own personal gain. John recorded, *"he was a thief; as keeper of the money bag, he used to help himself to what was put into it."*

Did John know this about Judas from the beginning, or begin to suspect his actions over time, or discover it after Judas had died. The Bible does not say when he had this epiphany about Judas, but John was very clear about the character behind the life of the betrayer.

Another insight into his character is indicated by a dialogue between Judas and Jesus in the Book of John. During a meal, a woman broke a very expensive jar of perfume over Jesus in her worship of Him. There, the Bible records that Jesus' friend Mary took a large quantity of expensive perfume, poured it over Jesus' feet, and wiped His feet with her hair as an act of worship. John wrote that Judas objected. *"Why wasn't this perfume sold and the money given to the poor? It was worth a year's wages"*.

Though his intentions seemed pure, John states, *"He did not say this because he cared about the poor but because he was a thief."* Judas fully intended to skim the funds from the money bag. Rather than expose Judas, Jesus responded to the supposed concern. And, at the same time He very poignantly addressed His own impending death, for which Judas would be partially responsible. *"'Leave her alone,' Jesus replied. 'It was intended that she should save this perfume for the day of my burial. You will always have the poor among you, but you will not always have me'"*.

Judas was anything but honest. Eventually he sold out Jesus to the Jewish leadership for only thirty pieces of silver – hardly a king's ransom. But the King of Kings was betrayed by a man who had lived and learned from Him for over three years. Judas only had financial gain in mind. His death is indicative of how he held no value for life, even his own. He can almost be pitied for his lack of faith and propensity for deceit.

Evil begets evil.
Infamous for his deeds, Judas was never able to overcome his legacy.

In the boat that night with the rest of the twelve disciples, Judas would have no doubt been thinking selfishly about his own survival. Possibly rowing with all his might, Judas would have expected to eventually make it to their destination with his money purse intact if nothing else.

When Jesus showed up to rescue His disciples, like the rest of them Judas was also likely greatly afraid. The text literally says that they "shrieked out loud for their lives." Judas more than the rest of his associates would have been possibly the most frightened due to his real lack of faith in anything spiritual or in Jesus Himself.

Judas was a master of deceit and mistruth. He only cared about financial gain, and even when he was at risk of being discovered would readily feign a masquerade of sympathy. It's not possible to really know how the other disciples felt about Judas, as no real text has been written in the gospels about his life other than what John wrote about his lack of morality.

The Bible records that at the moment Judas decided to betray Christ, Satan entered into Him. This demonic possession is proof that Judas had no desire to have a spiritual relationship with either Jesus or God. He was being Jewish by birth, not by religion. He would have avoided the devil if his desires were pure.

Because a foil was needed by Satan to attempt blocking God's plan for the redemption of mankind, Judas was the most probable candidate. The betrayal of Jesus had been long prophesied for hundreds of years. Judas was the lynchpin to make it happen.

There is an alternative story about Judas that has surfaced over the past few decades that is found primarily in a lost "gospel of Judas" ancient manuscript written in Coptic Egyptian text in the fourth century. This supposed story was found in a cave in Egypt in the 1970's and then eventually made its way to a collector of ancient memorabilia.

Deciphered in 2006, the story line says that Judas was actually on a secret mission from Jesus to allow this disciple to be the hero of the story. Unfortunately, even the traditional church writers of the time dismissed this writing as gnostic mysticism. This book never made it into the Biblical canon.

The Gospel of Judas does not display a historical reality, unlike those gospel accounts in the New Testament. Rather, this story line appears more like an alternative mystical tradition that was present in the Middle East during the time of its writing. Gnosticism was and continues to be geared toward a pseudo-spiritual, mystical element versus a true physical representation of Jesus and His disciples.

Even in ancient Biblical days of the New Testament era, there were some who felt that Judas was not really a traitor, but that he was one of Jesus' favorite disciples who was given inside information. Only Judas supposedly was given that special supernatural insight by Jesus into a spiritual realm that was exclusively shared with the disciple.

But fortunately, church fathers from those days who were given the task of creating the New Testament found that there was no empirical evidence for the validity of Judas' gospel. Not only that, the rest of the Gospels written independently by Matthew, Mark, John and Luke have no corroboration of the claims made by Judas in this "lost gospel."

His nature was never in line with the mission of Jesus, nor was Judas ever interested in a spiritual Kingdom of God. He, like most of the nation of Israel, wanted to get rid of the Romans. He thought Jesus was the person to accomplish that goal. When it appeared that wasn't going to happen, Judas looked for other ways to enrich his wallet. Even the thirty pieces of dirty silver he obtained from his dirty dealings with the dirty religious crowd were a way for him to enrich himself apart from the rest of the disciples.

From the very beginning he was a hypocrite. His life in general and in principle was a lie. He even gave himself over to be the willing host of the father of lies. Can you imagine the inner spiritual, mental, emotional and physical turmoil he must have felt those hours before he kissed Jesus in his feigned love. No wonder he never fulfilled a destiny outside of insult, pain and death.

Even the rabbis that paid him that paltry sum must have been laughing up the sleeves of their robes at him. Judas had been taken for a fool, and he finally realized it albeit way too late. He had served as their tool for evil mischief. He had traded salvation for sin, purpose for pity, faith for falsehood, life for death and a halo for hell. For the rest of time, Judas Iscariot would be regarded as the most tragic of all men.

Judas changed his mind and tried to return the money he received from the Jewish priests for his betrayal. But they refused to take it back. It was, indeed, blood money. However, his guilt was so great that he committed suicide. Judas was guilty of a terrible life and a terrible end. What a life lesson.

Being sorry is not the same as repenting from sin.

Being sorry makes you feel sorry for yourself. Being only sorry can either cause you to justify your sins or to suffer despair. Repentance makes you sorrowful that God was offended by your behavior. As a result you are driven to Him to receive His undeserved forgiveness – God's grace and mercy are bestowed on those who repent, not on those who just feel sorry for their attitudes and actions.

Judas was guilty of significant sin, yet at the same time he was a significant part of God's plan for the pathway to the redemption of mankind through his betrayal of Jesus. Everything he did, and everything you do, are part of God's will in His sovereignty over all of creation. Judas was responsible for his own actions which resulted from his decisions, but God used those missteps by this broken disciple to provide salvation for everyone who has ever lived before and after the crucifixion and resurrection of Jesus.

Maybe one of the most significant things that can be accused of Judas Iscariot was that in feeling sorrow for his crime of betrayal, he did not seek to atone for his sin with Jesus whom he had wronged. Instead, he went to the Jewish religious hierarchy, his accomplices in crime and thereby sought to set himself to be made self-righteous in false repentance.

The priests he had served in his selfishness failed him at the end of his life. Repentance was not within him to gain nor within them to grant. His life and death are a sobering example of poor choices and selfish desires.

Turning your back on God has severe everlasting consequences.

Chapter Seventeen – The Follow Up

What exactly happened the night of the story described in Matthew 14? On the surface, it's a story about faith and the miraculous power of the Son of God. But there are deeper meanings, just like what lies under the surface in any good tale of men struggling against the power of the sea and the winds. However, in this case, the struggle involved a spiritual power over creation and lessons of obedience.

Jesus gave a direct request for these followers to cross the Sea of Galilee and meet Him on the other side for time at their primary residential area, Capernaum. He was tired. All day He had been preaching, healing, and forgiving sin. He wanted time alone to pray and to be refreshed with one on one time with His Father. Jesus went up to the mountain by the sea to be alone with God. How often when you get tired do you long for the same personal time with Him?

The day before the fateful boat trip was full of activity. Miracles would happen, and lives would be changed. The Jewish world would be rocked by Jesus. His statements to the masses as well as to individuals were groundbreaking, shocking, captivating and beyond understanding to the population. The crowds that followed Him were greedy, but not for knowledge and understanding. They wanted more than spiritual nourishment. They wanted food.

Jesus was undoubtedly exhausted. He had a long day. Matthew's Gospel account in Chapter 14 is full of activity. Jesus had just learned that Herod had John the Baptist killed after having him arrested and thrown in his prison. Remember, this itinerant evangelist known for eating honey and insects, living in the wilderness, and calling out sin was related to Jesus. They were cousins through Jesus' mother Mary and John's mother Elizabeth.

The story of John the Baptist is an entire history of its own, and there are many more ways to spend time learning more on his life. For the purpose of the relationship between Jesus and John, suffice to say they were very aware of each other.

John recognized Jesus as the Messiah as soon as he saw him, and he baptized him. John the Baptist had a personal relationship beyond blood kinship. They were spiritually connected. John was the forerunner to Jesus, and he was calling those around him to receive Him as the long awaited, prophesied Messiah.

That scene in the Jordan River took place at the beginning of Jesus' public ministry, and is documented in the Gospels as a monumentally spiritual event. It was His official launch date to the world. Jesus obeyed the Father. The Holy Spirit showed up in tangible form. God spoke out loud.

His voice echoed from the Heavens that His Son is now blessed and to be followed. The trinitarian element of the Godhead was being manifested in plain sight. John the Baptist was the facilitator. John the Baptist and Jesus had a history together.

Matthew described the moment when Jesus heard about the death of his cousin. He most likely was deeply disturbed and emotionally drained. He had an immense sadness about the way it happened and the loss of kinship. Satan had used Herod to commit the horrific deed of murdering an innocent life. He was a pawn in the devil's scheme to bring an end to the one calling for repentance by all who sinned, including Herod and all his royal household.

Jesus was looking for a way to find solitude to deal with this tremendous personal loss, and he was hoping to find a place that allowed him to privately grieve and to rest from the non-stop onslaught by large crowds that were always chasing after Him. Jesus needed some Me Time, but it was not to happen at least that day. He was besieged by the thronging masses to be healed and have their needs met. The Bible said He had compassion on them.

All day long He was meeting needs, and finally they needed to be fed. Matthew continues his narrative by telling the story of what happened next. Five thousand men, not to mention possible women and children, had gathered together. They were tired and hungry, but there was no food or money to buy it for that many souls. But Jesus knew He could still satisfy the physical demands of hunger.

He wanted to teach the disciples a lesson about faith and God's provision. He also wanted to bless the crowd.

Can you imagine the scene? Thousands of individuals sitting around waiting to be fed. Only a small offering of a few fish and a little bread was available. The faithless dozen wandering around looking for solutions and unsure what to do or where to go. Jesus was the answer. As the Creator of life, He was divinely inspired to miraculously expand the quantity of food beyond reality.

First, He requested the offering be brought to Him. Then, He instructed the people to sit down in orderly manageable groups. Next, He asked His Father to bless the food and thanked Him for what was given. Suddenly, Jesus began to multiply the fishes and bread so fast that the disciples were struggling to keep up with distributing it to the thousands waiting to be fed. Finally, after every single person was fully satisfied with as much as they could eat, Jesus had created enough for extra meals to go.

This day long adventure on the Galilean hillside must have further stretched the humanity of the Savior. Although He was completely divine by nature, He was also completely human. How is that possible? No single person has ever been able to adequately explain this phenomenon except that it is one of the mysteries of God reserved to Him.

Man's finite intelligence can never understand the ways of God. As part of God's plan to redeem mankind from the penalties of sin and death, Jesus was the answer at the time. He is still the answer today to a lost and dying world.

Once this miraculous event had been completed, Jesus dismissed the crowd. He was ready to call it a day and seek the solace He desperately craved. Jesus needed to spend time with His Father to be both physically and spiritually rejuvenated.

He had been dealing with significant stress, lack of physical rest, emotional turmoil, the crush of untold demands by the people around Him, and disciples who were just still not understanding their roles and His truths. That's why He gave instructions to the disciples to leave that evening and meet Him on the other side of the Sea of Galilee.

It was an honest request, but it would have eternal consequences.

A long day for the twelve and for Jesus would turn into a long night for them. Matthew recorded that once they left, so did Jesus. He went to a private location on the mountainside near the lake to pray. He was there alone for several hours into the nighttime. Being refreshed by His Father was what He needed at that moment in time. He sought privacy and longed for conversation with God.

Meanwhile, a trip that should have only been a two or three hour voyage for the disciples had turned into a waking nightmare for them. This very simple task had turned into an almost catastrophic situation. For many hours, the "wind was against them." These strong men could not make any progress.

Their situation was indeed dire. When Jesus was finally restored, He was their answer. Had He not been able to spend time with His Father, He would have no doubt not been strengthened for the task at hand. Spending time with God provides strength for your journey.

Jesus was following up His commitment to His disciples after His commitment to spend time with His Father. As One who has infinite knowledge, He knew that His physical limitations could only be restored after His spirit was renewed. For that, it was critical that Jesus have the privacy of being alone with God. His spiritual life had been greatly stressed that day. His physical life was almost spent. Exhaustion takes a toll.

By getting away from everyone and everything, Jesus had the ability to get renewed unlimited power. The distractions of the day had limited His ability from a physical perspective. Once refreshed by God, He would soon perform another miracle. Walking on water is impossible, except for supernatural beings. When Jesus walked on top of the water and into the wind without restraint, He showed the disciples He was in control.

One ironic aspect of this nocturnal water adventure on the Sea of Galilee is how it ended. Keep in mind the disciples had been toiling all night long and were exhausted to the point of giving up. Not only that, but the sheer fear of seeing a creature of some unknown source approaching them like a poltergeist was altogether overwhelming for them. Only one man dared to test the water, and he barely survived it. Only one Savior was there to provide safety and comfort after identifying Himself to His followers.

The Bible records that once Jesus entered the boat with Peter and calmed both the Sea and the wind with just His voice, they were immediately at their original point of their destination. Another miracle in yet a string of miracles that proved that their Master was indeed the Son of God. These men were wind whipped, soaked to the bone, beyond tired and afraid, and incredibly confused with what they had witnessed that night.

It is said that the morning makes all things clearer. Did they understand what they had experienced with Jesus, or were they still unsure of themselves and of Him? Perhaps each man would consider himself lucky to be alive at the end of their jaunt on the deep blue sea. And perhaps they were second guessing their individual relationship with Jesus. Certainly, these twelve had a comraderie among themselves, but it was often tenuous. The Messiah was the one constant in the entire three years they traveled together. He is the One who held them together.

Even though He spoke with a voice of authority, their choice to continue in a relationship with Jesus was stronger than most of the others who were following Jesus for what they could get from Him. Peter especially felt something different after that adventure on the Sea of Galilee.

He knew that there would be more opportunities to learn, to serve, to minister, and to secure his position in the new Kingdom of God he heard so often spoken about by this teacher. He just didn't know how his part would be played out until sometime later.

Storms cause fear. Moments of failure come from faith lost in periods of uncertainty. You may be purposed to flee when your beliefs are challenged. Those conditions create a fight or flight mentality. You can choose to fight against the difficulties created by your life's storms with the spiritual strength that Jesus gives through divine empowerment.

The Holy Spirit works in you and through you, enabling you to stand strong. Or, you can choose flight, and run away crushed in your spirit, lacking confidence, wisdom and loss of faith in divine intervention.

Peter went through both during his life with Jesus. His victory, though, was allowing his faith to be restored. His storm had an impact on his life, and all those who knew him. With help from His Savior, he was able to rise above the waves and live a victorious life. Can you say the same?

Like Peter, when you practice following Jesus, getting to the other side of the storm provides a lifetime of lessons about belief and faith.

Chapter Eighteen – Row, Row, Row Your Boat

When Jesus approached the Twelve, they had been fighting the waves and the winds all night long. They were exhausted. They didn't have time to be distracted, and they were in a hurry to get to the other side with the hopes of not drowning. Can you imagine going for a ride on open water in a small watercraft, then out of nowhere have to deal with the possibility of dying?

Due to the topography of the area around the Sea of Galilee, storms can develop in a matter of moments. The hills that surround the lake provide a perfect conduit for winds that can suddenly create terrific waves that can easily swamp a small boat. These men knew the dangers of being caught on the open Sea, and the fishermen in the crew knew that all could be lost if they were unfortunate to lose the battle with the forces of nature.

The cold air that can come down from the 2,000 foot elevation, given enough time, can fall onto the warm air at the lake level, and the water can churn like a washing machine gone mad. After the sun sets, and the temperature drops, the hills around Galilee can create a perfect scenario for disruption of an otherwise clear body of water.

The boat they would have been rowing would have had an overload of weight with all of the men on board, and the waves could have easily started coming over the sides. The average small fishing boat in Biblical days would have been about 8-9 feet wide and 25-27 feet long. They would have had a shallow draft and not been too terribly deep. Typically, they would have also had a thin mast with a sail.

The standard boat in these days, typically used for fishing or light duty sailing, had only a small number of passengers or crew. It would usually sit about two and a half to three feet above the water line. When you load about a dozen full grown men, the weight of all those people drops the gunnels of the boat to about one foot above the surface of the lake. That's a big difference when a storm blows up. The chances are pretty good that the waves and water might swamp the boat and turn it over throwing everyone into the deep.

The boat still floats, but it would be more sluggish when it moved because of the weight of the extra passengers and the resistance of the water against the more expansive surface area of the boat below the water line. Additionally, the men would have been frantically rowing to make up time. The average time to move across the lake from one side to the other, especially in the direction the disciples were headed, was about two hours. In Matthew's account, the twelve were at it all night long, perhaps for almost eight to ten hours.

In 1986, archeologists found an ancient Galilean boat, also known as the Jesus Boat. It was discovered on the north-west shore of the Sea of Galilee during a drought when water levels receded. It is an ancient fishing boat from the 1st century AD, and although there is no evidence directly linking the boat to Jesus and his disciples it nevertheless is an example of the kind of boat Jesus and his disciples, some of whom were fishermen, may have used.

The story that Matthew wrote tells that the disciples had been fighting against the storm for hours, and what should have taken about two hours at the most was now stretching into the wee hours of the morning. Because the winds that whip up the water occur under certain weather conditions and only at the western end of the lake near Capernaum, it was likely they were almost to their destination before the difficulty arose. Nonetheless, it was a life and death situation for them.

Is there a reason they just couldn't get to their destination in the usual amount of time? Well, the storm was bad enough that it would not allow them to make any progress. Can you imagine being in a small watercraft designed for a small group and now have not only the weather turn against you but time as well? No wonder they were frantic. Some of these men were seasoned fishermen and used to uncomfortable situations. But this was different. The situation was ridiculously difficult and dramatically fearful.

Interestingly, it was just a short time before dawn by the time Jesus walked across the Sea of Galilee to these dozen men struggling throughout the night. He came walking to them at three in the morning, a time when most people are sleeping. These twelve were definitely wide awake, and they had been that way all night long. Evidently, they hadn't made that much progress after they had launched out from their departure point.

With supernatural sight, Jesus had seen the disciples struggling. Mark's version of the event in Chapter 6 of his account says that Christ saw them: *"And he saw them toiling in rowing."* Through the darkness of the night, the distance, and the windstorm, no other human would have been able to see their boat.

The big lesson to Believers here is that even if you lose sight of Jesus, He never loses sight of you.

As the disciples continued to row, their effort was in vain. That's part of what makes His approach to them so phenomenal. By any normal means, they should have been moving away from Jesus when He was approaching them. There were more of them in tandem working on one common goal to get to safety. They were all involved. The boat should have been making at least some movement forward, but they were stalled in place.

Christ was about to reveal Himself to these ship of misfits in a very powerful way. Everything about Jesus coming to His disciples was so magnificent - His timing, the manner in which He carried it out, and the direction He went. There was nothing hurried about it. Nor was Jesus taking a hazardous chance. The picture that Matthew paints is that Jesus simply willed to be with His disciples. No obstacle could stand in the way of His will.

Chapter Nineteen – The End Game

What did Peter need more than anything? Was it to believe in a Savior, or in a magician? Was his faith just temporary, or was it based on something more long lasting? Why was he the only one that felt compelled to step out of the boat when Jesus called him to meet him on the water? What were the other eleven disciples thinking? How do Peter's actions make him the one whom Jesus entrusted to build His church?

When Peter saw that Jesus was real and not a ghost on the water, he wanted part of that wave walking action. Maybe he felt he could perform miracles, too. Maybe he thought that he was special and that the rest of the disciples would admire and respect him more. Perhaps he felt empowered to be more than a mere mortal by defying the laws of physics and nature itself. Would he himself be like a god if he could walk on water?

Regardless of Peter's motivation, he wanted to be more like Jesus. The problem was that he looked at his surroundings more than being focused on the One who could save him from his fate. After all, didn't he just hear the Savior say to just "Come On?" In the text, Peter still wasn't sure who he was seeing was really Jesus. "If it's really you…." sounds like a very unsure phrase to use when you're getting ready to potentially drown in the middle of a huge lake at night.

Peter's faith in himself was likely more solid than his faith in Jesus. Admittedly, there is a certain element of trust that he needed to place in Jesus. Even he was smart enough to know that water doesn't hold grown men. Keep in mind that the sea was pretty riled up due to the storm he and his compadres were in, and it didn't appear to be getting any better. Winds were howling. Waves were crashing. The boat laden with twelve adult males was probably taking on water.

If Peter was thinking that he could nonchalantly exit the boat by hopping over the side and nonchalantly stroll over to someone else who was just casually standing on the surface of the Sea of Galilee, then he may have felt that he was dreaming or having some sort of out of body experience. How could he justify leaping over the edge of his safe but soggy surface onto a roiling body of water that was fourteen stories deep. That's a long way to sink to the bottom if he was wrong or if Jesus was just taunting him in a dare.

Peter's actions were death defying. He must have realized that if he was wrong, or if Jesus was out of His mind or lying, that he would surely die. There would be no other options, unless Jesus was telling the truth. Somewhere in the middle of Peter's thought process were elements of both sincere trust and absolute fear. He wanted desperately to believe that he could actually walk on the waves and not sink underneath them. He had a sole desire to know truth and trust the One who was speaking it.

Jesus had yet to change Peter's name to Peter which would happen at a point not long after this watery episode. He would be rock solid in the establishment of Christianity after the Resurrection and Pentecost. But there was a lot of ground to cover before that happened. Yet, Peter also knew that he would sink like a stone if he was mistakenly overzealous in his need to feel fulfilled at this moment.

So long as Peter depended on God and God's power, Peter was able to walk on the water as well. When Peter stopped depending on God, and tried to do it under his own power, he sank. Later in the Peter's life, after the resurrection and the ascension of Jesus to Heaven, he began in earnest to live for Jesus. It was at Pentecost that he came into his own, and thereafter he served as a true witness until his execution at the hands of the Roman government.

Peter's name for millions of Christians, especially Roman Catholics, is historically tied to the City of Rome which tradition has held for over 1900 years was the burial place of Peter. Images of him are everywhere there, and the sixteenth century St. Peter's Basilica was built over the spot where he was reported to have been martyred by Emperor Nero.

It commemorates his death. Church tradition going back to the fourth century tells about how and where he died. He was reported to have been buried in an ancient Roman necropolis after being crucified upside down.

Israel has a very different image of Peter. He was a fisherman from Capernaum on the western shore of the Sea of Galilee. Jesus nicknamed him Cephas, or Peter which meant rock, but his original name was Simon, or Shimon in the Hebrew variation. Twice he was referred to as Simeon.

Most of what is known about him comes from the New Testament including the Gospel accounts and the Book of Acts. Those stories provide the best image of the one the Jesus referred to as the "rock." Contrary to popular belief, it wasn't Peter's name that would be the foundation of the church, but the truth of the gospel upon which the church would be built.

Peter's personality was perfect for this small band of followers who stayed close with Jesus during His ministry. He was typically the spokesperson for them, the loudest and boldest, and often the most inclined to open his mouth and speak before engaging his brain. Peter was close at hand at almost every event where Jesus was involved with people.

He liked to see himself as the protector and leader of the disciples, and he knew there was definitely something incredibly special about Jesus from the beginning. It just took him some very humiliating experiences before he completely understood Jesus the Messiah.

However, Peter had some debilitating issues when it came to standing up for Jesus when it mattered the most. During the night of Jesus' trial after the last Passover meal, even though he showed incredible boldness by using a sword to defend Jesus at His arrest in the Garden of Gethsemane. Peter doubted. He hesitated. He swore an oath multiple times of his ignorance of his relationship with Jesus. He failed outright in his faith.

All of the disciples had their individual shortcomings. As a group, they weren't much better. Strength in numbers was not indicative of this assembly of followers. Yet in spite of these remarkable failures, Jesus made it clear that Peter would eventually be the leader of all of them as the heir apparent to proclaim the gospel to the world.

Each of the New Testament Gospels give a varying description of Peter, but they are all consistent in the basis of his special relationship with Jesus both before and after the crucifixion and resurrection. Peter would go through deep waters before rising to the occasion. He would be troubled because of his actions, but then triumphant in his restoration. He would be ridiculed for his disbelief, but then redeemed for his newfound commitment. He would be paralyzed with fear, but then would be promoted by a promise of faithfulness.

Peter would find strength after Pentecost to preach the good news to thousands of new converts. He would see his role expanded and his responsibility increased. He would find a new resolution in the redemptive power of the cross and hope in the resurrection. He is reformed from a common man to an astute proclaimer of God's message of salvation.

He would be made theologically astute and have supernatural abilities given him by the Holy Spirit – the power to heal and perform miracles. Neither imprisonment, accusations by religious authorities, or persecution deterred him from his ministry.

God opened Peter's eyes to see the world around him was greater than just Judaism and Jews. The divine call to take the gospel to the Gentiles was indeed visionary. He was pushed out of his religious comfort zone to reach people regardless of their place of origin or their religious affiliation. Peter was in a sense the original missionary to both Jews and Greeks.

How is that even possible? Peter's transformation began when he first met Jesus, and it was completed when he realized his spiritual power through the relationship he had with all three parts of the Holy Trinity – God the Father, Jesus the Son, and the Holy Spirit.

Peter's faith started out small, but it grew over time. By the time he was in full blown ministry as described in the Book of Acts, Peter was the spiritual giant of his day.

God's grace given to Peter through the miraculous touch of Jesus on the shore of the Sea of Galilee after the resurrection provided him the spiritual resource to restore his faith in himself and in the One whom Peter had denied just a few days prior to their breakfast encounter. Without the conversation between them to bring Peter back to faith in Jesus, the rest of the disciples may have meandered hopelessly forward without a new leader to guide them in their spiritual development.

They, too, needed Peter to be strong. They looked to him as the person who most likely would lead them to newly found spiritual insight and strength. The disciples reassembled around Peter. Without him, these men would have lacked the direction to begin ministering on their own through the power that God was willing to provide to them. The violence of the crucifixion was so overwhelming, they may not have survived the defeat without a leader who could instill in them the lessons that Jesus had been teaching them while He was on Earth.

Christ was the message, but they needed a messenger who could inspire them. Peter was that guy. If Peter could survive all the emotional turmoil he faced during his experiences with Jesus and be restored to full faith, then there was hope for each of the disciples to carry on themselves. His testimony became so strong that even the Apostle Paul referenced his relationship as a key influencer in the early church. Peter was the dynamo for years that kept Christianity moving forward and expanding in the growing population of that day.

Peter began using a Greek variation of his name, calling himself Cephas. Paul was able to establish a personal relationship with Peter, and for the most part were friendly with each other. There were some disagreements between them over Jewish religious customs, but those seemingly were resolved and didn't destroy their mutual respect for each other.

Interestingly, Peter's faith continued to grow as a result of his affiliation with Paul, especially over the issues regarding circumcision, sharing food with Gentiles, and the concept of salvation in Christ for everyone. Those were theological and cultural hurdles that Peter eventually overcame.

As strong as Peter's personality was, he was not a solo act when it came to sharing the spotlight. He was always part of a group effort. Once again, after the church was gaining ground in Jerusalem, Antioch and other key cities in the eastern Mediterranean area, Peter was a key counselor in many important decisions.

He was known to be chief among the early pillars of the Christian movement. When the church expanded beyond Jerusalem to Rome, Peter was considered a primary source for taking the gospel to Europe. Both he and Paul as contemporaries were instrumental in promoting the early Christian message to Gentiles.

The end game for Peter was his not his martyrdom, but his position with Jesus as the natural choice to spread the gospel after the ascension of Christ to Heaven. Peter's life after that point was totally devoted to establishing the message of salvation through a personal relationship with Jesus. Peter represented his faith out in front of the masses to which he preached. He led by example once his restoration was completed in Jesus. His life meant complete sacrifice to self. Peter showed full commitment to the mission of spreading the good news of Jesus, death, burial and resurrection. Christianity, even in its infancy, had a hero.

The Way, as it was originally called in the first century, had several thousand converts from Judaism and pagan religions. But by the middle of the fourth century, it is estimated that the rapid growth of the Christian religion had grown to roughly 30 million people.

It is a very shareable religion, based on a personal relationship with Christ. Another key factor that helped institutionalize that early faith and its growing community of Believers was the conversion of the Roman Emperor Constantine in 350 A.D. His recognition and proclamation of his newly found faith provided a major impetus to spreading the gospel.

Today, Christianity is reported to have over two billion followers around the globe, and it continues to grow. In spite of persecution in some areas, faith in Jesus is exploding in countries that historically have been resistant to the Christian religion. Protestantism, Catholicism and other denominations of the Christian faith have some fundamental differences in doctrinal beliefs, liturgical and ecclesiastical practices, and other varying ways to worship and practice faith.

For example, Catholics pray to Mary the mother of Jesus and to various saints for multiple reasons, which has no Biblical basis. Their belief in purgatory, or a halfway waiting room before Believers go to Heaven upon their death is an idea not grounded in scripture. Other matters too trivial to pursue here are more traditional in nature from long centuries of church practice.

Many of those ecclesiastic positions found their genesis during the dark ages in Europe when the general public was grossly uneducated and fearful. The masses unquestionably obeyed the authority of the church which ruled with an iron fist, and often the intermarriage between royalty and popery was so close that the lines blurred over the power struggle between them. Ignorance reigned supreme.

Pontifs for hundreds of years commanded with absolute authority, and the people blindly and willingly subservient followed suit – until a German monk challenged the status quo. Thus, the Reformation was birthed.

Yet, there are some similarities in general Christianity. At the core is the common belief in Christ as the only way to salvation. You have Peter to thank for that. His counterparts also played supporting roles in their apostolic positions within the early church. Once Pentecost happened, there was no looking back. These men were supercharged with the Holy Spirit, and they began to make an immediate impact on the lives of everyone with whom they came in contact.

As a result, they all suffered the pain of martyrdom except for John who lived the longest, eventually dying from old age albeit suffering at the hands of the Roman government for decades as an outcast. As each of these followers of Jesus lived and died, their message of salvation which began as a flicker has become a roaring flame in the succeeding millennia.

The end game for Christians is found in the eternal message of hope and an everlasting faith.

Chapter Twenty – What's the Point

Jesus was making a statement on the Sea of Galilee. He was showing the Twelve that followed Him that He was in control—over nature, over time, and over them. As God, He was able to move time and space to accommodate His purposes for the disciples.

Although they didn't know it at the time, these men were about to have an encounter with the Creator of the universe and of the world in which they lived. What they saw as a supernatural phenomenon, Jesus was providing a front row seat to His ability to suspend the natural elements of wind and water.

When Peter stepped out on the water, he was held up by the power of the spoken word of the One who spoke the world into being. He created the water, and so He could cause its properties to obey Him. He could make gravity disappear, and it would support the natural weight of a fully grown man who would be weightless upon the water's surface.

Peter's faith to step out of the boat, knowing he could possibly die by slipping immediately under the waves to his certain death, became the second part of the miracle. When he left the boat, Peter started out with good intentions. Unfortunately, his faith faltered.

Nevertheless, Peter's leap of faith did not end in failure.

Initially, in his own confidence he felt the waves under his feet, but then he took his eyes off Jesus. He quickly looked to the wind and the water – everywhere except to his Savior. Even in his fear, though, Peter cried out knowing that Jesus was the only one who could save him. When Believers take their eyes off of Jesus and focus on their difficult circumstances, they begin to sink under the weight of their problems.

The first part of the miracle was the fact that Jesus Himself walked across the lake, likely at a miraculously fast pace. There is a possibility that he moved there by suspending time and space, thereby showing up exactly when He was needed. Keep in mind, the Christ wanted the Twelve to struggle so that they would appreciate His power and begin to understand the reason for their faith and trust in Him beyond earthly leadership.

When Jesus called to the disciples across the water, and His words were filled with tenderness: *"Be of good cheer; it is I, be not afraid"*. Not only was He saving them, He was teaching them. Three individual parts of His words were full of lessons. First, He encouraged the disciples: "Be of good cheer." The literal meaning in the original is: "Take courage." Their courage had vanished. Here He tells them to take fresh courage.

Secondly, Jesus revealed Himself as God. That was the reason they should be encouraged. In short, Christ was telling these men He is the great "I am." This self-revelation of Jesus to them is the calm within their storm. He has the power over men and nature.

Thirdly, He consoled them. The first part of what Jesus told them was a positive command. This last part of the phrase is a negative command: *"Be not afraid."* It is as if He brought in courage and cast out fear, and all because He is the Messiah, the Anointed One, the Word, the Savior. His statement was designed to calm their fears and their spirit. He knew that these twelve men who were diligently awaiting His presence, although not expecting Him to show up on the water in the middle of the night, were all fearful men who needed Him.

Jesus needed to display His divine nature to these spiritually handicapped humans in order to strengthen their faith in Him. Otherwise, they would continue to doubt and argue and fight against His clear and concise teaching, not because they were naturally pugilistic, but because none of them had ever stepped beyond the boundaries of traditional Judaism. They were bound up by the law, and Jesus was teaching them grace. Their Jewish minds were blown every time when He would perform a miracle. He wasn't a showoff. He was God.

The cornerstone of faith is belief.

That belief can be in someone or something -- in a power greater than yourself or something supernatural that defies explanation. These dozen doubters were continually stumbling in their faith in Christ, and it was only when He showed up on top of the Sea of Galilee that they slowly began to see Him in His real light, the Messiah – the Son of God.

Jesus sought to assure His disciples in their fear. However, He was primarily proclaiming and confirming the nature of who He was and is. Jesus was not a ghost hovering over the water to surprise them with theatrics. He walked across the water on sandals. His credibility was His claim to be the very Creator of the sea on which He stood. Nature got it. The disciples finally got it, although they were a little slower to understand than the wind and the water.

Not only that, but Jesus told them who He was to assuage their fright. He used the same words that His Father used with Moses in the wilderness. "I Am." They each would have understood that phrase. It was no misuse of the term that every Hebrew youth had heard in the temple and in their homes when studying the Torah. The Books of Moses were crystal clear about that name – the name of Jehovah God. And Jesus had every right to use it.

Can you imagine being in that little boat and seeing a raging torrent water that was ferociously slapping the sides of your craft to the point of sinking suddenly become smooth as glass? What about the howling wind that immediately ceased, not just die down a bit at a time. It flat stopped when Jesus said so. White caps became calm water. Waves became ripples. Wind became calm. Who could do such things? Only God. The dramatic element was so profound, that the disciples instantly declared their belief in Jesus as the Son of God.

Jesus was at once concerned about both their physical and spiritual needs. He showed that to them just a few hours before when He fed thousands of people with only a small basket lunch. He presented them the opportunity to stretch their faith and feed their appetite at the same time. He was concerned about their safety in the storm, and their spirit when they feared the worst. He saved them from both destruction and denial. He was genuinely interested in providing both protection and provision in all their needs.

Jesus cared for them, and He cares for you.

Jesus is not a God who is unaware of your fears, failures, and faults. Jesus is not blind to your spiritual or physical needs. His is compassionate and merciful towards those under His care as He reaches out His powerful hand of salvation. As when He reached out to Peter to save him from certain death, He reaches out to all who call His name to rescue them. Fear and doubt can be released, and belief and faith can be restored.

Jesus performed these miracles to give the disciples just a glimpse of who He really was. The twelve may have intellectually understood that He was the Messiah who had been prophesied to come, but they were clueless that Jesus will lay aside His divine power in order to give up His life on their behalf. This sovereign King goes from whipping the wind into shape, to being crucified on a cross in order to bring about the redemption of His people.

This story is not a metaphor. If it was you could discount the entire New Testament. The event is told as an actual account, so it must be seen in that light or dismissed with the rest of the scriptures. Those documents can be assessed regarding reliability just like any other historical document. Just say for a moment you have decided they are accurate. In that case the question is not 'what is the meaning' but, 'why did Jesus do this'.

Another account of this incident in Mark's gospel includes this phrase, *"He was about to pass them by…"*. Then immediately after this passage about Jesus walking on water, Mark says this was done, "because they didn't understand about the loaves and fishes…". Although a slightly different version, the perspective was an indication of their lack of faith. He told them what to do, but they were once again being stubborn.

Peter exhibited bold behavior and display of his faith as he went to Jesus out of the boat. However, he still could not keep his fear at bay in order to stay afloat. Like all men, Peter was plagued with the depravity of human nature. Peter's lack of faith was a clear exposure of every human's lack of ability to command the world's natural elements. He was incapable of defeating anything including his own fears. In contrast, Jesus showed Himself as victor over death, fear, and nature itself. The Creator commanded creation.

Jesus delights to deliver you when you call upon Him for salvation. Salvation in Him does not come from being righteous or from working hard. Jesus didn't come as the King of Kings so that you could have everything you desire. He did not come to make you wealthy, famous, or comfortable.

Instead, Jesus entered into the world and humanity to show Himself as the way, the truth and the life. He walked on water so that everyone may know Him as God in human form and glorify Him. His incarnation led to His death, which led to His resurrection, which leads to salvation to anyone willing to believe.

Believing in Jesus does not leave you unchanged.

Believing in Him develops you into a disciple who is faithful to proclaim Him and glorify His name. The same Peter that sank in fear and later denied Jesus three times is the same Peter that founded the church in Jerusalem. Jesus both saved Peter from his sins and moved him to share His faith with others.

Many people are religious, but their faith, hope and trust are in their own ability to be good enough, follow the right rules, know the right things, say the right words – dependence not on God, but dependance on self. Individuals deceive themselves into thinking they are following God. Those people are not following God. They are doing as they choose, as they think it should be for them.

That is the very way everyone has failed from the beginning. It's the very same sin that Adam and Eve committed in the Garden. They thought they could eat the fruit God commanded to not eat, and everything would be ok. They did as they thought. They were surprised when it did not. Disobedience has a price. Lack of faith has negative results. Disbelief deters and defeats belief.

Every person who has ever drawn breath has the same reality that Peter experienced. Sin and shame leads to sinking into depression and death. As you call out to Jesus as Lord and Savior, He is quick to reach out His hand to rescue you and save you from certain death. Jesus walked on water in order to provide a path to Him. Even when Peter denied Jesus, he was restored.

Even when Peter went back to his old job after the resurrection, Jesus gave him a new purpose. Even when Peter was hesitant and embarrassed when Jesus questioned his faith, he regained his courage and his belief in Christ. Jesus can do that all for you, too.

Chapter Twenty-One – Wave Walker One

When Jesus met the Twelve on the water during their long day's journey into night, He did so with His customary miraculous way, knowing that unbelief was sure to cause a forward leap in faith by the disciples. He knew that by suspending gravity for Peter, and by sustaining the ferocity of the storm that these men would want to know Him more rather than leaving as soon as they came ashore.

The real question is, however, if their faith was emboldened enough that night to cause immediate salvation or serve to strengthen their resolve to follow Him without doubt not knowing Him as a Savior or the Messiah, but as a leader with extraordinary powers and insight. Although Jesus was God in the flesh, his humanity was what they saw, and not His divinity.

Impressed at His ability to suspend nature, they were not fully aware of His real purpose and divine nature. At the point in time of the Galilean boat ride, the Twelve were still clueless to the power and majesty of Jesus and His divine relationship to His Father.

Although the apostles had started their boat toward Capernaum, the storm deflected their course. The language of the text suggests that they probably came to land at the south end of the plain, somewhere near Magdala, and made a circuit of the cities in the plain of Gennesaret at the western end of the lake on their way to Capernaum. Plans change, and the disciples even struggled with that. They were planning to go home, but Jesus caused them to go back to work in an area they didn't know or didn't like to do things they didn't want to do.

Beyond these issues of faith and obedience, the Twelve were dealing with some genuine feelings of hard heartedness. These men had just witnessed the miracle Jesus performed of feeding thousands of people by using a very small amount of food. He blessed it, multiplied it, and then had them distribute the loaves and fishes to everyone who had more than enough to eat, and then had more than enough leftovers for another meal.

They still didn't get it. Jesus miraculously manipulated the atoms which made up the food to increase it for consumption by over 5,000 men, not to mention women and children. Some scholars believe there may have been three to four times as many people including them. It's like they just didn't want to believe He did that right in front of their eyes. Talk about being blinded by the Light.

Their hearts were hard to realize the implication of just who Jesus really was; if they had realized it, then they would not have been surprised by Him walking on water. For the Twelve, the miracle just before this boat trip that Jesus did in which He multiplied the food was not enough for them to realize just how much power and authority He had. These men were operating on a scope that wasn't connecting all the dots in spite of seeing it happen first hand. A hardened heart is one where truth or belief doesn't penetrate.

Their minds were dull to understand the miracles of Jesus. Comprehension of what they were experiencing wasn't getting all the way to top floor. This does not mean that they were in opposition to Him, but simply that they were slow to grasp the significance of His power. The disciples were slow to learn, as they ought to have known, that the Messiah was omnipotent—He had all the power, and He could therefore stop the storm and allay their fears.

Jesus walking on water and Peter's attempt to join Him is certainly a story of faith and courage. However, if you look at the narrative from the point of view of an Israelite of Jesus' time, the story will get whole new layer of symbolism. Jews from Jesus' time were very familiar with stories from the Torah and also highly aware of prophecies made by the Prophets coming true. Peter and the disciples saw Jesus as the Messiah, but they were still in disbelief until after the resurrection.

Jesus almost never made the claim to His divinity. However, He would occasionally drop hints. Jews of His time would be sure to understand that Jesus was claiming to be the Son of God. Feats like forgiving sin and accepting worship are just two of these sometimes not so subtle suggestions.

Walking on water in fact actually relates back to Genesis 1:2: *"The earth was without form, and void; and darkness was on the face of the deep. And the Spirit of God was hovering over the face of the waters."* Nor is walking on water just a magician's trick. Rather it is Jesus telling His disciples (and indirectly readers of the Gospel) that "Hey, it is me, your God!"

The disciples would have wondered at nothing which Jesus could do within the whole scope of His limitless love, grace and power. The glory He manifested in His miracles failed to illumine their minds, and in spite of seeing them on a daily basis, the Twelve lacked divine understanding. Were they that stupid? Why couldn't they discern what was happening to them and others literally right before their eyes? If the disciples were not grasping the reality of who Jesus was, it was their own fault. No wonder He kept referring to them as "ye of little faith."

Jesus chose the twelve men to walk with Him during His ministry on Earth. They were uneducated commoners. These simple men of faith gave up everything to be His followers. He spent three years training them to be leaders. His eventual plan was to charge the disciples to take over and carry on the work He had started. Jesus chose ordinary, unrefined men to be his disciples. They were uncommonly common. He purposely passed over the socially elite, aristocratic, and influential. Jesus selected mostly men from the bottom rung of society. God's economy has worked this way for thousands of years.

He didn't want followers who were solely interested in getting and not giving, selecting and not serving, leaving and not loving. Jesus knew these men from the inside out. The only one that really lost in the end was the one destined to do so from the beginning. Judas Iscariot, the odd man out, was divinely appointed to be part of the dozen who would change the world but do so in a way that caused one of the worst days on the planet but the best day for mankind.

Two thousand years later, Believers still have hardened hearts. Although the Bible has been around in its current form for over 400 years, people don't like to admit that miracles still happen today. For so many centuries after both the canons of the Old Testament and New Testament were established in the fourth century, people relied on the church to tell them what and what not to believe. Ignorance became an art form, and only the educated in the church hierarchy were allowed to have access to the Scriptures.

After King James took the bold step of getting the Bible interpreted into English and published for the masses in the early 1600's, the faithful slowly began to read and interpret the Bible for themselves. Yet, even after all those centuries, most individuals have no clue about what the Word of God says.

People continue to be ignorant of the Biblical knowledge available to almost everyone.

With the availability of the internet and smart phones, anyone anywhere in the world can get access to the entire Bible for free. You don't even need a hard copy of it anymore. It's that simple. But it's oh so hard for most men and women who refuse to ask for divine wisdom, who are too lazy to read, or are just too hard hearted to accept the truth of God's Word. And many are still faithless, in spite of seeing answers to prayer in their own lives.

The concept that mankind has wrestled with since the days of the life, death and resurrection of Jesus is to understand just who He was and is today. For the disciples, He represented faith, hope, trust, love and more. They were willing to die for Him, but realistically only after He rose from the dead.

Prior to that, they only gave it lip service as they each shrank away in the night after Jesus' arrest after their last Passover supper together. They were afraid. They had lost hope. They all were in total, utter disbelief. It would take the resurrection to make them see the light.

Two millennia after Jesus walked by the shores of the Sea of Galilee and rode in boats on the Sea of Galilee with the disciples, and the calmed the Sea of Galilee with His voice, men and women are still struggling with faith, hope, trust, love and more. Most people want the easy fix, or the softest blow from injurious behaviors. They shrink in belief, and they run from God when disobedience takes the forefront in their lives.

Like Adam and Eve in the garden after they tasted the forbidden fruit, people are quick to blame others for their troubles. The first man and the first woman were guilty, and they knew it. That has not changed for thousands of years. How else do you explain tragedy upon tragedy in the world?

Evil exists, and it comes in many forms. There is only one creature that provides it in its purest form, but mankind is responsible for acting it out in all types of forms. Jesus made a way to overcome it. He is the One victorious over it. His followers today can change through Him. Faith in God through Him is the answer.

Why did the gospel writers include the story of these Wave Walkers? What does it represent, especially today during what appears to be a post-Christian world? In Scripture, the sea usually referred to sin, death, and judgment, going all the way back to the beginning ages in Genesis when God cleansed the earth of wickedness during the time of Noah and the flood.

During the Exodus, God allowed His people to cross the Red Sea unharmed on dry ground, but when their enemies followed, He destroyed them under the water. The sea roared back at His permission to remove the fear and disbelief that the nation of Israel was experiencing.

In the Old Testament the sea is used often to symbolize tremendous uncertainty, insurmountable difficulty and sometimes wickedness due to disobedience. The prophet Micah wrote that the sea is the place where God sends sin to be forever judged, forgiven, and forgotten.

Yet, His promise to Believers is that He is going to one day make all things new and wipe away all those terrible images and feelings that cause fear, doubt and unbelief. Jesus today stands above the sea as One with authority over it all as He did that night on the Sea of Galilee two thousand years ago.

The greatest story ever told is about Jesus.

The Sea of Galilee is one small but powerful story in His life on Earth. During His public ministry, which most Bible scholars agree was about three and a half years, He accomplished so much that John writes that, *"Jesus did many other things as well. If every one of them were written down, I suppose that even the whole world would not have room for the books that would be written."*

In the course of about 1,200 days, Jesus gathered a small group of followers, taught and preached to large crowds in various towns and cities, performed amazing miracles, cast out demons, healed those who were sick and diseased, and spiritually and socially interrupted the traditional religious society.

He made such an impact on the Jewish community that their ecclesiastical hierarchy sought to have Him arrested, tried and put to death. Of course, they would fortunately have the Roman government provide the way and the means of execution so their hands would not be dirty.

During the entire course of His ministry, Jesus would be continually teaching His disciples. He constantly talked with them speaking with compassion, but occasionally would be frustrated with them. A few times He even was angry at their stupidity, ignorance, and lack of faith. More often than not, though, Jesus would be disappointed in them, not as individuals, but for how they constantly exhibited a lack of faith in Him and in His Father.

These twelve men left all their familiar surroundings to follow a man they did not know with only one single phrase, *"Follow Me."* The disciples one by one were chosen by the Messiah to join Him on a grand adventure. Their time together was an incredible series of teaching moments stretched out over a small handful of years, but their time spent together had eternal consequences, not only for each of them but for the rest of mankind from that point on til now. Difficult? Yes. Impossible? No.

When He began His ministry after His cousin John the Baptist ("the baptizer") baptized Jesus, most scholars agree that it was about 27 A.D. He was about thirty years old as noted by Luke in his gospel, and His death on the cross was in about 30 A.D. There is some ambiguity about exact dates, and as a result historians and theologians use approximate windows of time to calculate when Jesus was alive.

Some of that credibility is based on historical evidence of what was happening in the area during those days, and some is based on scriptural texts. Although they are not completely exact, the events establish a general timeline of when He was ministering during his adult life.

Jesus was more about obedience to His Father than training uneducated men. However, the time He spent pouring Himself into the disciples was part of His obedience to God. He was given a mandate to provide salvation, and that message was to be carried out by those He hand selected. Before the foundation of the world, God had proposed an eternal plan created specifically for all mankind. Jesus was the conduit for its activation.

When Adam and Eve sinned in the Garden of Eden, God already knew they would. He had given them the choice to obey Him. But they chose disobedience instead. For thousands of years men and women have been forced to live in a world that has been on a downhill slide since their fall. All of creation itself has been groaning as a result. One day, however, redemption of the entire universe is going to happen. Jesus plans to be there. His Father already has the plan laid out.

Jesus chose men who were open to wanting more. Each man had the desire to know more about how they could each change their world. All but one eventually did. And he was replaced by another one who did. The stories told by them and about them are inspirational, motivational and eternal in consequence. The disciples spent their time with Jesus trying to figure out ministry, and they frequently stumbled. He told them what to do. Sometimes they listened, and sometimes they had their own ideas.

These singular enigmatic followers were slow to catch on, but Jesus had chosen them for a specific purpose. He knew who they were, and He knew what they would become. During the Last Supper, when the time had come for Jesus to fulfill His destiny, He spent several hours together with them. Alone in an intimate setting, He provided incredible insight into what He wanted them to know as His last teaching moment with them. In their final hours together, He was concerned for them and their eternal destiny. He never gave up on them.

John's gospel records the detailed conversation between the disciples and Jesus. Before they left the room, He prayed for them. Interestingly, he repeats in His prayer to God His Father what He had told them before. Typically, in Biblical times, Jewish men would seek a rabbi out and request to be a taught as a private student. In this case, the opposite took place. That concept was counter to the culture of the day when rabbis would only accept the brightest young men who petitioned them to be students tutored in the Hebrew faith.

The seventeenth chapter of the epistle of John displays the love that Jesus had for the twelve men who had been His closest companions. The entire passage is His prayer for them:

"After Jesus said this, he looked toward heaven and prayed:

"Father, the hour has come. Glorify your Son, that your Son may glorify you. ² For you granted him authority over all people that he might give eternal life to all those you have given him. ³ Now this is eternal life: that they know you, the only true God, and Jesus Christ, whom you have sent. ⁴ I have brought you glory on earth by finishing the work you gave me to do. ⁵ And now, Father, glorify me in your presence with the glory I had with you before the world began.

⁶ "I have revealed you to those whom you gave me out of the world. They were yours; you gave them to me and they have obeyed your word. ⁷ Now they know that everything you have given me comes from you. ⁸ For I gave them the words you gave me and they accepted them. They knew with certainty that I came from you, and they believed that you sent me. [9] I pray for them. I am not praying for the world, but for those you have given me, for they are yours.

[10] All I have is yours, and all you have is mine. And glory has come to me through them. [11] I will remain in the world no longer, but they are still in the world, and I am coming to you. Holy Father, protect them by the power of[b] your name, the name you gave me, so that they may be one as we are one. [12] While I was with them, I protected them and kept them safe by[c] that name you gave me. None has been lost except the one doomed to destruction so that Scripture would be fulfilled.

[13] "I am coming to you now, but I say these things while I am still in the world, so that they may have the full measure of my joy within them. [14] I have given them your word and the world has hated them, for they are not of the world any more than I am of the world. [15] My prayer is not that you take them out of the world but that you protect them from the evil one. [16] They are not of the world, even as I am not of it. [17] Sanctify them by the truth; your word is truth. [18] As you sent me into the world, I have sent them into the world. [19] For them I sanctify myself, that they too may be truly sanctified.

[20] "My prayer is not for them alone. I pray also for those who will believe in me through their message, [21] that all of them may be one, Father, just as you are in me and I am in you. May they also be in us so that the world may believe that you have sent me. [22] I have given them the glory that you gave me, that they may be one as we are one— [23] I in them and you in me—so that they may be brought to complete unity. Then the world will know that you sent me and have loved them even as you have loved me.

[24] "Father, I want those you have given me to be with me where I am, and to see my glory, the glory you have given me because you loved me before the creation of the world. [25] "Righteous Father, though the world does not know you, I know you, and they know that you have sent me. [26] I have made you known to them, and will continue to make you known in order that the love you have for me may be in them and that I myself may be in them."

He never gave up on any of them. Only one gave up on Him. Temporarily they ran and hid, were fearful and doubt-filled, ridden with anxiety and concern for their own welfare after the crucifixion and before the resurrection. After that, however, once Jesus restored them to full faith, these men were all out for the sake of the gospel. They never looked back. Their lives became testimonies to the love they had for Jesus and the desire each of them had to fulfill the last commandment He gave them before He left them and returned to His Father.

From a religious perspective, the disciples were slow in their spiritual development before the resurrection. When Jesus ascended to Heaven forty days later, these men woke up to the realization that it was their time to turn the world upside down for the gospel. They had been in training for three and a half years. The last instructions were definitive. Peter, James, John and the rest of them finally got it.

They were the original Christians – Believers who finally believed.

Two thousand years later, Jesus is still concerned over the eternal destiny of every person on the planet, and everyone who has ever been born and lived since then until the present day. What Believers know and practice today in large part is a lifestyle that is primarily based on scripture. They read the Bible. They pray. They meditate. They go to church. They listen to sermons. They participate in small groups for Bible study.

During the COVID pandemic they learned how to watch religious services on live stream and television. And, in some instances those Christians who are the most faithful in their commitment to be involved on a regular basis maintained some sense of participation.

All over the world, Believers can become more like Jesus if they so choose. The scriptural account of the faith of the disciples and their relationship with Jesus is a model for modern Christians to follow. To imitate them is to become more like the Messiah they followed.

Life is hard, and often it is made harder by personal choices that do not coincide with the instruction of God's Word.

Belief in a higher power or supernatural source can be sincere. However, it can be sincerely wrong if not focused on the right Person. For those who do not know God on a personal level, faith comes when God calls you through His Spirit, your belief in Him becomes than head knowledge, and it is finalized in a personal acceptance of Jesus in your life. There is no other way for anyone to secure a permanent relationship to God or to have a life after death in eternity with Him. Heaven is the destination. Jesus is the Answer.

When the storms in your life are about to sink you, overwhelm you, and cause you to lose faith, remember that your miracle awaits in focusing your attention on the One who calms the storms, rescues the dying and brings salvation. What is your choice today? I hope you choose life everlasting.

Acknowledgments

God's Word is rich in content, and it speaks to Believers when they wish to hear. He wrote through prophets, through disciples, through missionaries, through priests, and kings. What is incredibly amazing is that sixty-six books written by all these different individuals over thousands of years all point to one incredible story.

The Bible is the story of how God interacts with man from the beginning of human history until today. His words live not only on the page, but also in the lives of those who have a personal relationship with His Son, Jesus Who is called the Christ.

My journey began at the age of sixteen, when I handed my life over to Him at a youth camp on the Ohio shores of Lake Erie during the Summer of 1971. At an evening rally and service with lots of other teens in attendance, for the first time I heard and understood that I was in need of a Savior.

I went forward during the invitation, met with an adult counselor, and prayed to ask Jesus into my heart. It sounds so simple, and yet that moment was so profound as it was the beginning of my spiritual journey.

Now, don't get me wrong. I was not one of those kids that was wild and unruly, who drank and smoked and slept with girls. I was raised in a home that had Christian parents, who went to church every time the door opened. I grew up in a small Methodist church in my hometown in Southwestern Pennsylvania, and I never did anything wrong (at least in my own mind.)

I'm sure my parents would have disagreed a little, but as the oldest of six children, I was expected to be the good child, the leader, the one that my younger brothers and sisters were to look up to all the time.

But, I realized that at as a teenager, during that hot August evening, I needed to know that if I died, that I would end up in Heaven. I also recognized that I couldn't do it on my own, in spite of my own goodness. As many kids who grow up in church, I thought that I was doing everything right and had it made. When my spiritual eyes were opened at that camp, I suddenly understood that I needed a God that could save me from myself, from Hell, from the world's evils, and keep me safe in Him.

Now, over fifty years later, I cling to that promise even more. What I also am grateful for are a loving wife and two great kids that help keep me centered. When I feel that I am all that, they have a way of bringing me to my senses. My wife Connie is very good at making me realize that it's not always all about me. My daughter Emily and my son Logan are able to help me focus on Who is really important.

They all love me, and I love them—more than words can really say. For them, I dedicate this book about God's love, His forgiveness and faithfulness, and how much His Son provides us with saving grace when He is Savior and Lord. They all know that well, and they each experienced that special time when they became Believers. For that, I am eternally grateful.

A life apart from God's love is no life at all.

We are closer as family because His Spirit lives within each of us. We are quicker to forgive when we get upset with each other. We are more inclined to seek forgiveness than hold a grudge too long. We love each other more deeply because we are bound in His love. And, we pray, a lot. And, yes, we are very involved in church and its ministries. I am glad that we are as it gives perspective on life.

We are able to help others and minister to people in ways that non-Believers usually don't understand. Jesus asked His disciples to love Him and to love each other. Sure, we each struggle with each of those commands, yet our family is strengthened when we pull together in tough times and celebrate even more in good times. Families love, and Christian families love even more.

I pray that this book helps you feel the need for both faith and salvation. Faith is good, but it has no eternal significance without the personal knowledge of faith in Jesus Christ. "For under heaven there is no other name where you can be saved." Regardless of what any other religion espouses, the truth is that you need Him. There is no other alternative.

For these reasons, I dedicate this book to my wife Connie, my daughter Emily, and my son Logan. I love you!

Reviews – What Readers Say About

"Wave Walkers"

"Mark Roberts has done it, again. In his book "Wave Walkers", Mark recounts one of the most dynamic stories in the New Testament of Jesus and His disciples. A story that illustrates the storms we all face and how we, with our eyes on Jesus, can make it to the other side.

You will appreciate the nuances of the background of the story, the historical significance of the setting, and the insights into the lives of the followers of Jesus. Most of all, you will see how Jesus walks with all of us, never abandoning us in the storms of life."

- Dr. Bob Miller, Ph. D, D. Min, Executive Pastor of Operations, Florence Baptist Church, Florence, Kentucky.

"In *Wave Walkers*, Mark Roberts introduces the Twelve who dared to follow Jesus. *Wave Walkers* provides a fresh look at Jesus and His disciples. And if you look with a sharp eye, you may discover a fresh look at yourself glimmering back at you. So, don't miss the boat! Become one of the *Wave Walkers*."

- Dr. Bruce McCoy, D.Min. AVP of Development, Southwestern Baptist Theological Seminary, Fort Worth, Texas.

"It worked. Mark exhorts us to "think about how you can insert yourself into the story now to be told." I felt like I was in the boat fearing for my life through the storm; terrified by the ghostly figure approaching the boat; and then dipping my toe in the water by faith taking that step.

Mark's book does a phenomenal job representing the life and times of the disciples giving us a fresh view of these first followers *who turned the world upside down (Acts 17:6)* for the cause of Christ. It renewed my desire to do the same. Perhaps it will yours as well."

- Rev. Dr. Dan Allen, DD, Executive Director of 800FollowMe and Joy in Jesus Ministries, Telford, Pennsylvania. (In Memoriam).

"Mark obviously did a mountain of research on the twelve disciples, so you wouldn't have to, and then applied it to one of Jesus' miracles. This is an indepth treatment regarding "walking on water" and how it applies to following Jesus. A great deal of work and deserving of your time."

- Dr. Mark Hine, D. Min., EVP of Student Affairs, Liberty University; Superintendent, Liberty Christian Academy, Lynchburg, VA.

"'Wave Walkers' is not a book about theory or pie in the sky religion. It is about the wisdom and experience of Mark Roberts. It is in truth how the story of Peter walking on the waves became a living, breathing truth for Mark. It is about his walking from belief to the testing of whether those beliefs can play out in reality. Thinking you will make it through when the great tests of life come must be tested. Will you look to Christ or the waves?

Mark obviously loves history and so gives a deep, rich context of where this miracle happened. He makes the characters involved, real people. They are not just historical figures but people with jobs, relationships, struggles and face life like each one of us. Mark takes you from what you say you believe, often theoretically, and moves you to a living, breathing, walking faith experience with Christ.

I know Mark and have had coffee with him regularly over the last few years. What I know is, this book is a mirror of his life as he faces and struggles through the stuff of life. I know 'Wave Walkers' will change your life as it has mine. Buy it for yourself and maybe a friend. Read it together and experience the challenges of life as you move from the shallow waters of simple belief to the deep waters where the waves can swallow you up and where faith is not an option."

- Mark R. Demos, CEO, The Legacy Forum, Dallas, Texas.

Wave Walkers

Wave Walkers - When Belief Becomes Faith

The author wishes to thank the following individuals who aided in their review and critique of the text and its content:

Dr. Greg Ammons, Mrs. Lisa Guillermin Gable, Dr. Bob Miller, Dr. H. Bruce McCoy, Dr. Dan Allen, Dr. Mark Hine and Mr. Mark R. Demos.

About the Author

Mark Roberts is a published author. His first book *"Going the Speed Limit – Seventy Character Lessons on Life's Highway"* was published in November, 2015. A second edition was published in the Summer of 2020.

The first edition of Wave Walkers was published in September, 2022. This volume is the second edition.

Mark has written over 600 articles on healthcare, leadership and sales, and has contributed to many magazine publications for healthcare. He is a licensed health and life insurance agent.

Mark lives in Dallas County, Texas. He serves as a deacon in his local church, and he is a loyal alumnus of his alma mater Liberty University.

Mark currently has several more books in various stages of development.